And

And

THE TINY WORD THAT CAN RADICALLY
TRANSFORM YOUR LIFE

Bree Rosenblum, PhD

Hearth Press
TAOS, NM

AND
Copyright © 2025 by Bree Rosenblum

Stories from the author's life have been represented as accurately as possible. Some names and details have been changed to protect individuals' privacy.

For permission to reprint portions of this content or bulk purchases, contact bree@breerose.com

Author Photograph by: Elena Zhukova
Published by Hearth Press, Taos, NM

ISBN
Hardcover: 979-8-9917530-5-0
Paperback: 979-8-9917530-0-5
eBook: 979-8-9917530-1-2

Library of Congress Cataloging-in-Publication Data on File at lccn.loc.gov

*For you, dear reader, may AND enrich your life
in unexpected ways.*

Contents

PART I

Encountering
AND

CHAPTER 1

From OR to AND

The Power of Little Words

What do all great leaders and lovers, teachers and trailblazers, pilots and performers, artists and athletes, inventors and influencers, monastics and magicians, surgeons and sailors have in common?

They all know how to transform challenge into creativity.

You can, too. All you need to do is shift a tiny word in your vocabulary.

OR and AND are words. Obviously.

But they are also ways of living.

This book is an invitation out of the constraints of OR into the possibilities of AND.

OR is all about rigid choices. *This OR that. Here OR there. Now OR later.*

OR is a master at pitting things against each other. OR is fine as a grammatical conjunction, but it's not so great for your life. A life ruled by OR tends to be rife with conflict, constraint, and compromise.

In contrast, AND is all about possibility. *This AND that. Here AND there. Now AND later.*

AND is a master at bringing things together. AND is delightful for crafting compound sentences, and it's also fabulous for your life. A life inspired by AND is full of creativity, connection, and capacity.

The tiny shift from OR to AND will have a radical impact on your life. It's not a simple magic bullet or a one-time offer expiring tomorrow. Instead, it's a new way of relating to yourself, others, and the world.

AND is a living, breathing companion for your ever-evolving life.

The Fallacy of Before and After

The OR-to-AND process I'll share with you is the result of decades of living, learning, traveling, and teaching in diverse contexts.

I'm a professor and a scientist, a coach and a facilitator, an author and an artist. I've worked in classrooms, coffee shops, and corporations. I've taught in museums, massage parlors, and meditation halls. In all these contexts, I've seen the same struggle.

My students and clients crave freedom but often feel crushed by the weight of the status quo—in their lives and in our world. They want to live profoundly creative and meaningful lives on their own terms. They want to lead their communities, classrooms, or companies to new horizons.

I imagine that you do, too.

I hope this book will be a companion and guide for your journey.

But let's be honest.

Any book that promises you a tidy "before" and "after" is smoking a pack of lies. We change. We evolve. We transform. That process never ends.

Most self-help frameworks are selling you a magical process to transform a miserable you into a happy you.

The problem is that it doesn't work. You—and your life—are constantly changing. Any static process is bound to fail. And when we don't achieve health, wealth, happiness, or enlightenment, we feel jealous, frustrated, betrayed, and inadequate. The feeling that something's wrong with us is actually heightened because we have failed once again to achieve a mythical "after."

Some self-help frameworks are more sophisticated and roughly follow a hero's journey. The hero leaves the ordinary world to go through a transformational journey. Now, instead of a single, life-changing event, we have a series of magical processes (and maybe a dragon) to transform a miserable you into a happy you.

A journey framework offers more depth (a complex hero) and realism (a road of transformation full of challenges, obstacles, and sometimes pain). But in the end, we are still stuck in the myth of the conquering hero. We think we need to leave home, learn something on the road, and return victorious. The better "you" is still off in the distant future. It's exhausting.

I'd like to propose a journey with a different shape. It's not a line, and it's not a circle. It's an AND.

I'm not going to draw you into the picture above because I don't know where you're starting, and I don't know where you're going. All I know is that you've got more in you than a line or a circle. You've got a glorious squiggle laid out under your feet, and you're ready to take the first step.

So, before we begin, can we agree to drop the lines?

Our lives and our evolution are not linear. We don't get a tidy before and after. We don't need starting lines, finishing lines, dividing lines, or coloring in the lines.

OR is a boring slash: /

AND is a curvy invitation: &

Let's see where it takes us.

Boxes, Bricks, and Books

When we start our journey with AND, we leave behind the lines. But we also quickly get tired of boxes.

Chances are, you've been outgrowing some boxes of your own.

What boxes? Could be anything. You may be breaking out of a dusty crate of constraint. Or a boring cage of conformity. Or a heavy chest of conflict.

Sometimes, you squeeze yourself into a job or a relationship or a persona that doesn't quite fit. You don't see another option, so you choose to make yourself just a little smaller and more enclosed.

Other times, a box gets built around you without your conscious choice. You wake up one day and realize that the walls of your life are pressing in. Your shoulders are crunched, and you crave a place where you can stretch out to your true size.

And it's not always so dramatic. You may not feel cooped up or penned in or knocked down. You may just be ready to fly around the wild, expansive territory of your life. *You don't need to be in a dungeon to value freedom.*

It doesn't matter if your box feels small or large, new or old, locked or open. You are ready.

It's time to live a life of great possibility.

We're here (the book and I) to offer you a way to transform constraint into creativity.

You don't need to shred your box into a million pieces with a utility knife. And you don't need to wait for someone else to free you. You can work with the conflicts and constraints you are facing right now in real time.

And here's the good news: Life is on your side.

Do you believe that? It's fine if you don't. You can change your mind at any time.

By the way, four of my favorite words in the English language are "*I changed my mind.*"

I've needed to change my mind a lot because I have been wrong about a lot of things. One of those was my belief that life was an indifferent and uncaring force, which is ironic because I'm a biologist. I literally study life for a living.

Give me nearly any species on the planet, and I will wax poetic about its beauty and purpose. I see majesty in the black-eyed Susan, the brown recluse, the lilac-breasted roller, the green tree frog, and the rosy boa.

But for the longest time, I just couldn't feel the deeper current of *Life Itself.* Sure, I knew that life was fascinating and precious, but it was still a lower-case word in my mind. I was wrong. Life deserves a capital place in our hearts.

Life is *alive.* It's not standing in the shadows indifferent to your fate. Life is constantly nudging you in the direction you need to go. Even the obstacles in your life are ready to reveal great possibilities. The question is whether you are ready to listen.

One of my most cherished teachers puts it this way:

> *If you aren't paying attention to the deeper currents of your life, Life taps you with a feather.*
>
> *If you still aren't listening, Life tries to get your attention with a brick.*
>
> *And if you still aren't hearing the call, Life hits you with a truck.*

Consider this book somewhere between a feather and a brick. Perhaps something like... a book.

If you're ready to listen to the deeper currents of your life, sometimes Life hands you a book.

So, here we are. Let's roll.

Hit on the Head

I'm not writing this book from some high horse, pretending I've always had it figured out. Let's start with when my AND journey began: a time when I wasn't listening, and Life literally hit me on the head.

One damp day in 2013, I was sitting in the muddy grass of a soccer complex in Albany, California. My five-year-old daughter was running around with her team on the field. My one-year-old son was in my lap, demolishing a burrito.

I had just started a new job as a professor at UC Berkeley, and I had barely made it to her soccer practice. I'd locked myself out of my office (again), so I was late to pick up the kids. Then I made the questionable decision of dropping my daughter alone at the field to meet her teammates while I ran to get food with my son. I plopped down on the ground behind our team's goal, thinking about how good my life probably looked from the outside.

Just that morning, my mom was gushing, "*It's so great, sweetie. You've got two beautiful children, a great husband, a new house, and a job at one of the best universities in the world. You've had such a wonderful life of adventure and travel... and it's just so great.*"

But inside, I was hanging on by a thread. I had just left my closest friends to move across the country (again), and I was playing the same stupid game of trying to be a Good Mom, a Good Wife, a Good Professor, a Good Mentor, a Good Meditator, a Good Friend, and a hundred other good things that I didn't even want to be. It was like being in a tug-of-war with too many ropes. I was spent.

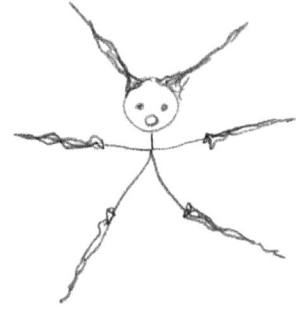

On the field, the soccer ball lazily meandered into the goal (because how often do five-year-olds score on purpose?). Ecstatic about the accidental win, my daughter's team piled into the goal with the other team close behind. A swarming sea of kids heaped on top of each other, pushing further and further into the goal, tugging harder and harder on the net, until...

The weight of the players tipped over the entire structure, and CRACK... the crossbeam crashed on my head.

Three things happened simultaneously. First, a rush of intense pain radiated from my crown. Second, I felt a flood of gratitude that my son hadn't been crushed. Third, I had a knee-jerk reaction to pretend I was okay.

I thought, *"Woah, I'm really hurt,"* but I managed to stand up, gather my kids, brush off concerned spectators, and drive home with silent tears streaming down my face.

The next morning, I forced myself to go to work. Because that's what I used to do: pretend everything was okay even if wasn't. I stumbled through the hallway until a colleague told me my eyes weren't pointing in the same direction. I shrugged off his suggestion that I go to a doctor because: (a) I'm stubborn, and (b) They don't do much for concussions anyway. But by the time I got home, the pain had caught up.

I relented and called an old friend who was a chiropractor. The next day, I was in his quietly lit office in San Francisco.

I'd never been to a chiropractor before. As my friend worked on the tender bones of my skull, I felt a lifetime of ignored sorrows, fears, and bruises clamoring for my attention.

After our session, he asked, "Bree, why did you get hit in the head?".

I started to tell him the story, "*Burrito, soccer goal, wrong place, wrong time.*"

He cut me off with emphasis, "*No, Bree. WHY* did you get hit in the head?"

The question was haunting. The signs had been there for months. A mismatch between my inner and outer world. From the outside, things looked great, but inside I was a mess of conflict, contradiction, and constraint. Maybe I was living someone else's perfect life.

As I gathered my things together, I noticed a red wooden "&" sign in the corner of the office. The ampersand stared at me.

I asked myself, "*Why did I get hit in the head?*" and the sign said, "*AND.*"

I thought, "*What is wrong with me?*" and the sign said, "*AND.*"

I pleaded, "*What am I supposed to do?*" and the sign said, "*AND.*"

I started to get a little infuriated. What kind of answer is "AND" to the big questions of life? AND isn't a roadmap. It isn't a compass. It isn't a self-help book. It's a single word and sometimes barely that: a shape staring at me for no reason.

As I walked past the office lobby, I noticed a flier by the door. My friend, the chiropractor, was teaching a course called "The Multidimensional Body" every Thursday night for the next seven weeks. I felt an inexplicable draw to the class but dismissed it immediately. I'm a scientist, not a chiropractor. Plus, I was already imposing on my family by being broken and taking time off from work by being useless. I felt selfish for even considering doing something just for me.

Because we all know that the Good Mother doesn't leave her kids. But if she does, it's for a very important work event that she simply cannot miss, and she makes an absolutely fabulous dinner in advance, so no one is inconvenienced, and she writes her children personalized goodnight cards with hand-drawn cartoons to remind them of her love.

There's simply no room for levity, spontaneity, or Thursday night classes.

The next day, I was resting on a simple wooden chair in my backyard, watching the shadows of the wisteria play on the ground, when I was overcome by a heart-stopping peace. Besides my day job as a scientist, I had long been practicing and teaching yoga and meditation and was friendly with the serenity of inner focus. But this wasn't Bree *feeling* tranquil. This was absolute peace—sitting down in my broken body, knowing with utter certainty that all was well.

I had spent years running a mile-a-minute to keep the ship ship-shape. And now I was sitting in the backyard doing nothing and being unreasonably happy.

Hurt and happy had always seemed like a solid "either/or." But what if they were actually a "both/and"? In a single wooden chair, there was Bree in pain AND Bree at peace. One was broken, and one was entirely whole. The shadows of the wisteria played, and the red ampersand returned to my mind. It said, "AND?"

I called and signed up for the Multidimensional Body class.

Over the seven weeks of the course, the red "&" kept patiently sitting in the corner. It wasn't staring at me with the stink eye anymore. It was inviting me on a new journey.

And that journey was both exhilarating and painful.

First, I needed to see how OR was running my life. From the outside, it looked like I was living a life of AND (I was a professor *and* a meditation teacher *and* a mother). But in reality, the things I cared about were in constant tension with each other. I was continually making choices that dug me further into conflict and compartmentalization, and I was exhausted.

Second, I needed to see how all of this OR was actually coming from me. My mind was an OR factory. Sure, there were external constraints in my life, but most of them originated with me. I was the one limiting my choices and wearing a deep groove of fear and OR in my mind. Humbling.

Third, I needed to learn a new way of thinking. Physically recovering from a brain injury takes time. It took months before I could read a newspaper or scan the dizzying array of milk cartons in the grocery store without becoming physically nauseated. But I wasn't just healing my brain. I was changing my mind: my assumptions, beliefs, and habits of thought. I was divesting from OR and investing in AND—from the inside.

Fourth, I needed to craft a new life that had a heart of AND. Any change of heart has tangible effects on our lives. It was time to step out of the boxes I had created and consider new possibilities in many dimensions of my life, from health to family to career to romance to spirituality.

The aftermath of this journey—the life I live now—would have been unfathomable to the overworked, overextended, undernourished, under-slept Bree sitting on the soccer field all those years ago. She knew her life looked good from the outside, but she didn't know that life could feel so good from the inside.

At the time, I wasn't listening to myself, so Life used a soccer goal and a little red ampersand to get my attention. The journey kicked off by that AND has been the richest of my life.

It turns out that AND is far more than an overlooked conjunction. AND is a roadmap, a compass, and a way of life. It's now also a little self-help book to guide your transformation from OR to AND.

I'll share more about my own journey in the coming chapters. But what's important now is *your* journey.

If this book has found its way to you, AND is ready to tango. Why not let it lead you onto the dance floor?

A New Friend

For me, it took many years to motivate and catalyze a transition from OR to AND. It took many more before I had a process that I could share with students and clients.

The good news is that those years of struggle and study led to a process and a set of practices that you can use in your life right now. In the coming pages, I'll offer you the strategies that I've found to be most meaningful and effective in my own life and for the people and organizations I work with.

The OR-to-AND process is general and holistic. It can stand on its own as an approach to personal exploration and transformation. It's also compatible with—and complementary to—any other path you're traveling. The types of inquiry we'll use can enrich and deepen your meditation, prayer, therapy, or art practice.

Our time together will be divided into four parts:

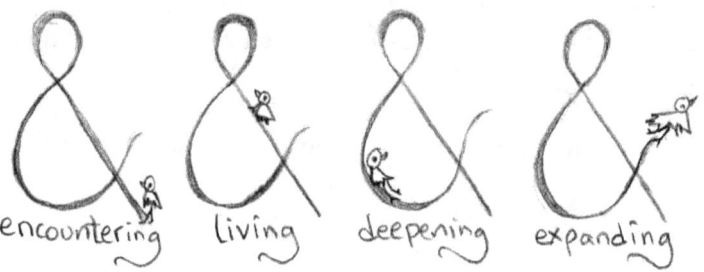

encountering   living   deepening   expanding

Part I – Encountering AND

You've already met AND. In the rest of this section, we'll look at the dangers of staying in bed with OR and the promise of living life with your new friend AND.

Part II – Living AND

I'll share the core processes I use in my teaching, coaching, and consulting to help individuals and organizations shift from OR to AND in how they think and how they live.

Part III – Deepening AND

I'll offer specific practices and exercises that can support deep transformation in your life as you begin to divest from OR and nourish AND.

Part IV – Expanding AND

We'll explore ways to expand and mature in your transformation and your life. AND will be by your side the whole way.

Throughout the book, I'll also ask you questions and offer chances for guided reflection. You don't need anything more than what you've got in your hands to dive deep. But if you'd like to rustle up a little journal or sketchbook, AND will be happy to help you fill it with new musings, insights, hopes, and dreams. And if you'd like a dedicated place for your AND explorations, I've got a companion guided journal just waiting to hop into your lap.

For now, sit back, relax, and imagine the wonderful horizon of living a life of great possibility.

CHAPTER 2

The Perils of OR

Lurking by the Bar

Before I introduce a process for shifting constraint to creativity in your life, I want to give you a proper introduction to OR and AND.

Imagine I've invited you to a party. OR is brooding in the corner, wearing dark sunglasses and a scowl. AND is kicking it up on the dance floor, wearing a nifty mismatched outfit and a quiet smile.

You arrive and give OR and AND each a quick handshake on your way to get a drink. It's a long enough party that you'll have time to circle around and get to know them in more depth. Even so, first impressions are powerful.

As soon as you walk into the room, you can feel negativity radiating from OR. Alone by the bar, OR is muttering, criticizing everything and everyone, and occasionally tripping people as they walk by.

You'd like to avoid talking to Oʀ and just head to the dance floor. But I insist. I want you to meet the sinister force lurking in the shadows. This chapter is your introduction to Oʀ. Don't worry, you'll get to meet ᴀɴᴅ next.

The Pitfalls of Oʀ

Oʀ is great as a grammatical conjunction. If I am going to paint your house, I'd want to know whether you like beige Oʀ fuchsia. If I am running a workshop for your organization, I'd like to know whether to expect ten Oʀ 10,000 attendees.

But, as a life philosophy, Oʀ is dangerous. A life lived with Oʀ at the helm is chock-full of:

- Constraint
- Compromise
- Conflict
- Compartmentalization
- Control
- Criticism
- Conquest
- Conformity
- Conventionality

When we are stuck in either/or thinking, we see trade-offs and constraints everywhere. We are constantly creating conflict—internally and externally. We think life is a game to win or lose. We try to control everything, and we criticize anyone (or anything) that doesn't bend to our will. We compartmentalize our lives and compromise our values. We are constantly afraid of making the "wrong" decision and often end up choosing what we consider the lesser of two evils.

And even with all that effort, we still live relatively conventional lives, caught in the jaws of OR.

OR makes us tight, afraid, and stingy with ourselves and others. OR divides the world into us OR them, friend OR foe. OR wants to feel pleasure without any pain. OR wants to take credit without accepting blame. OR cares far more about definitions and decisions than it does about joy and jubilance.

When we are stuck in either/or thinking, we become rigid leaders, stingy lovers, and intolerant global citizens.

OR might not be ruling your life, but I guarantee it's there, behind the scenes, limiting your choices in subtle ways. We slip in and out of either/or thinking moment to moment, day by day. So, even if you aren't facing a painful push-pull between different arenas of your life, you might find subtle ways you're holding back because of OR.

It's all fun and games until OR sticks out its foot and trips you at the party.

Let's look at some specific ways that OR constrains your life.

Pleasure OR Pain

A life of OR feels tight and narrow, like a stifling battle. Whether you are facing immense conflict or subtle friction in your life, OR is often the culprit. And before we can release OR into a nice, wild green pasture, we need to find out where it lives.

If you look closely, you'll find that OR lives in your mind. So, OR-living always starts with OR-thinking.

OR has gotten a little too comfortable in your head. It's hidden under a bunch of nice soft blankets, so you might not see it right away. But it's there. Look in the corner where you hide your most binary thinking.

Take the big polarities that we like to pretend—and almost unconsciously assume—are black and white:

- Good OR bad
- Right OR wrong
- Pleasure OR pain

Feel free to add a few more to the list.

Let's zoom in on pleasure/pain. I'm not denying the reality of pleasure or pain. I'm saying that we are locked into binary thinking about it. We want to define one box called pleasure and another called pain. We want to neatly categorize every experience into one of these boxes. And we want to say yes to what's in the pleasure box and no to what's in the pain box. We want all daffodils and no dead squirrels in our yard. All gooey cookies and no broken bones in our memories. All harmony and no war in our world.

There's no problem with having preferences or a desire for daffodils, cookies, and peace. But our preferences don't control reality. Just because we crave harmony, it doesn't protect us from the horrors of war. OR-thinking doesn't help us live happier, more fulfilled lives. It doesn't lead us to a more harmonious world. As hard as we try, we can't create a life—or a world—populated exclusively with pleasure.

Our attempts to avoid pain actually make matters worse because we are fighting reality, and reality always wins. So, when we attempt to elude pain and grasp for shreds of pleasure, we ultimately lose by avoiding vast swaths of our lives.

What's the alternative?

We need to move out of the conflict of OR into the courage of AND.

The good news is that OR-living starts with OR-thinking. And we have the power to change our minds. If we replace OR with AND, we arrive at a much more constructive—and accurate—understanding of the world.

The reality is that our lives contain pleasure AND pain. They aren't separate boxes; they are in *relationship*. You can think of pleasure and pain as being on a spectrum or overlapping each other or relying on each other or even being embedded in one another.

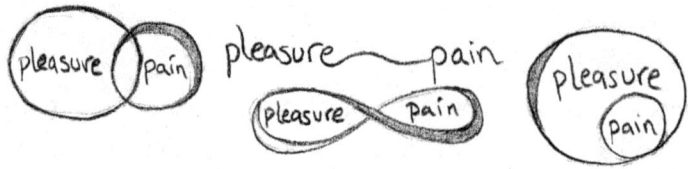

It doesn't matter how you view them. All you need to realize is that putting pleasure and pain in separate ironclad boxes is something *we* do. It doesn't reflect reality, and it doesn't benefit our lives.

When we put up a mental wall hoping to avoid pain, all we avoid is our lives. Once we put opposites back in *relationship*, we are free to move more honestly around the landscape of our lives.

The same is true for *all* binary thinking. For example, if you look closer, you can't put good/bad in mutually exclusive boxes either. You may tell me it's bad to push my son, but you might change your tune if I'm pushing him out of the way of oncoming traffic. This isn't a semantic trick. It's an example of how we lose context, nuance, and freethinking when we try to box up reality.

Let's be clear: I am not suggesting we throw out values, ethics, or morals. In fact, I'm proposing that we have far more character, conscience, and integrity when we are *paying attention to life* rather than feeding the beast of OR.

This OR That

Another reason we spend so much time in binary think-ing is that we are (consciously or subconsciously) trying to craft—and then maintain—a particular identity.

Would we be so judgmental about right and wrong if we weren't trying to be right all the time?

This brings us to the other big way that OR constrains our thoughts and our lives.

OR tries to bind us into rigid roles that it claims are mutually exclusive. Once OR has you convinced that you can only be "this" OR "that," it wins another medal to wear on its messed-up blazer.

Here are a handful of OR conflicts I've seen again and again in my students' and clients' lives:

- I can be a good parent OR have a successful career.
- I can choose a noble calling OR make a lot of money.
- I can be fiercely independent OR find a loving relationship.
- I can take care of myself OR take care of others.

Are there others that feel relevant to your life? Feel free to add to the list.

We might be able to imagine a wildly wealthy, free-spirited parent and entrepreneur who runs a nonprofit and has a loving partner. But when we look at *ourselves* and our *own lives*, we feel conflicted and constrained. We are drawn to people who seem to be living AND lives, but we don't know how to give the gift of AND to ourselves.

OR conflicts are not always about our hopes, desires, or dreams. They can also be about our secrets, beliefs, or fears. Again, here are a few themes that surface in my coaching sessions:

- I can work myself into the ground OR get passed over for a promotion.
- I can be a watered-down version of myself OR upset my family.
- I can placate my partner OR be in great physical or emotional danger.
- I can hide my past OR risk my reputation.

Here's a specific example. Recently, I had a coaching call with Anna, a phenomenally talented computer scientist. For months, Anna had been watching others subtly take credit for her work. Anna didn't want to appear pushy, so she slowly—and accidentally—started agreeing to a diminished reality. When she talked with her collaborators, she downplayed her accomplishments. When she gave presentations to the higher-ups about her progress, she started saying "we" instead of "I." The conflict was affecting her morale, her relationships, and her confidence.

The situation was coming to a head because Anna was being sidelined from an important project she helped develop. She was losing her seat at a table she built.

Anna had an authentic desire to get credit for her own work, but it was tangled up with a longstanding fear that she would be seen as selfish. A friend might have said to Anna, *"Don't worry, you're not being selfish."* A business coach might have suggested, *"Let's strategize about ways you could approach your boss.*" But neither option would have helped Anna move past OR into AND.

Anna needed to see the way OR had her backed into a corner. She had subconsciously created a conflict between her integrity and her safety. In Anna's case, it sounded something like, *"I can ask for credit for my work OR keep the peace with my colleagues."* And when OR threatens our sense of physical, emotional, or psychological safety, it usually wins.

But it didn't win with Anna. Anna ended up standing up for herself AND preserving close relationships with her colleagues. She just needed to address her deeper fears, which she accomplished with the OR-to-AND process I'll teach you.

Before we dive into the specific approach, let's make sure we're able to see the shady tricks OR is playing in our minds.

OR tells us to live in a tiny box where one desire is met, and the other is sacrificed. OR seduces us into believing a crappy story where we have to choose between the lesser of two evils. In Anna's case, she felt that she needed to demean herself to maintain a collegial workplace. Our mind can be so preoccupied with OR that AND is completely hidden.

OR takes root by twisting authentic desires into competing fears. Fear narrows our focus to one goal: Avoid catastrophe at all costs. Once we are in the clutches of fear, OR seems to be our only option.

OR leads to painful compromises and conventional choices. We think we are playing it safe, but we are really giving up parts of ourselves. OR offers a life where we access only half of our potential and live only half of our dreams.

What kind of life do we really want to live? Sometimes, to see the real costs of OR, we need to have a childlike innocence. Let me give you an example.

The 100 Percent Club

A few years after the Soccer Goal Incident, my daughter came into our small, cluttered kitchen with frustration pouring off her eight-year-old body. She plopped down at the too-small wooden kid's table, which I was setting with wine glasses.

I was getting ready for "Fancy Restaurant"—a game we played when I didn't want to cook. I was several years into the journey of releasing my need to be the consummate Good Mother, and Fancy Restaurant was a way for me to simultaneously entertain the kids and blow off steam.

The kids would sit at a finely coiffed table. I'd be the "nice" waitress who took their order, and I'd also be the "mean" chef named Boris, who rasped with vitriol every time he got an order and was prone to absurd outbursts. After pretending to be perfect for so many years, it was fabulous to have a time to act a little unhinged.

As I poured fake wine, Chloe said in a deflated voice:

"Mom, something bad happened today."

I immediately began imagining terrible possibilities. I reminded myself to breathe, listen, and wait.

It turned out to be run-of-the-mill bad—a painful interaction with a classmate. As she recounted the details of the story, I breathed a sigh of relief. I arranged bananas with peanut butter on plates, and we discussed ways she could handle the situation.

A few minutes later, Chloe piped up again:

"Mom, wouldn't it be great if I could fast forward through all the hard times? I'd never have to be mad or sad or hurt or anything."

I looked up from chopping strawberries to respond but paused when I saw her face change. The frustration was draining, and she looked stricken. Before I had a chance to say anything, she gasped:

"Mom, I'm basically saying that I only want to live 50 percent of my life. That's a terrible thing to say! Why on Earth would I want to avoid half of my life before I even know what's going to happen?!?"

Out of that moment, the 100 Percent Club was born.

After I served dinner (as the nice waitress) and cleaned the kitchen (as the curmudgeonly Boris), we talked (in kid terms) about what it would be like to experience 100 percent of our lives. Not just the pleasure but also the pain. Obviously, we wouldn't seek out pain, hurt, frustration, or disappointment. But when those things came our way, we'd remind each other that we were part of the 100 percent club.

When I set up Fancy Restaurant in our dingy kitchen, I was already creating a space of AND. And in that space, the cost of OR was apparent.

We never made T-shirts or membership cards, but that evening offered a powerful inspiration. If an eight-year-old could see the cost of avoiding life in such stark terms, so could we all.

Yes, pain is painful. We don't have to *want* it. But it's never too early—or too late—to cultivate an authentic relationship with the totality of our lives.

A Tired Story

I'll have more to say about *how* we can move from OR-living to AND-living, but for now, I just wanted to introduce the danger of OR. Before we learn to live a life of AND, we need to see what OR is costing us.

To be honest, I wanted this chapter to slightly exhaust you. I wanted you to feel the weight of OR—how it limits your thinking, constrains your choices, and stifles the creativity of your life.

OR is telling you an old, tired story. And tired stories are, well... tiring. In OR's story, you are limited, constrained, and doomed to painful trade-offs, difficult choices, and disappointing outcomes.

Ultimately, an OR life is a 50 percent life. An AND life is a 100 percent life.

Let's talk about how to get you to a life full of AND.

CHAPTER 3

The Promise of ⒶND

Onto the Dance Floor

Imagine we're back at the party. You've managed to extricate yourself from OR's shady corner of the bar, and you're making your way over to meet AND on the dance floor.

As soon as you shift your attention to AND, something wonderful starts to happen. It's like you finally remember that you're at a *party*. It's supposed to be fun and interesting.

And no problem if you're not that into parties. Maybe it's an intimate dinner. Or an afternoon with your cats.

Regardless, AND is there asking why you're still wearing your soggy, heavy coat?

Your cloak was protection against the elements on your way here. But now you've arrived. Take it off and stay a while.

As you unbutton your coat, you start to feel decades of constraint, criticism, and conflict loosen.

O*R*-thinking is like a heavy coat. It's an *outer layer* of protection. O*R* created a persona that it thought would help you survive in the world. But it's not you.

Have you ever picked up a jacket loaded with rocks?

I have. My son loves rocks. As he walks through his day, stones seem to magically jump into his pockets. By the end of the winter, his jacket must weigh thirty pounds.

That's what it's like with O*R*. You are laden with days of stories, years of fears, and decades of other people's expectations. You've developed coping strategies to deal with the weight.

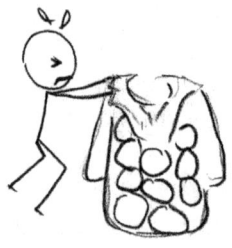

A*ND* wants to know what happens if you take off the coat and empty its pockets.

A*ND* wants to know who you are without the cloak and doesn't care if it looks pretty. A*ND* doesn't mind if your hair is disheveled or you've lost a sock or you need to cry for days before you even consider stepping onto the dance floor. A*ND* has infinite patience to find out who you really are.

A*ND* also has a head start on getting to know you. A*ND* knows that your true self is full of possibility. How does

AND know? Because AND knows an awful lot about reality. It turns out that AND is one of the most powerful concepts in the universe and the foundation of our very existence.

The Possibility of AND

So much of what matters in our world is the result of things coming together in new ways. In fact, you owe your very life to AND.

You wouldn't exist without the fusion of egg AND sperm. Your blood wouldn't move without hydrogen AND oxygen colliding into water. Your lungs wouldn't breathe without oxygen atoms coupling into O2 (yes, even oxygen needs AND).

And don't even get me started on the formation of planets, solar systems, and galaxies. AND is the fundamental creative power of our universe. Whenever disparate things come together, they spawn incredible possibilities.

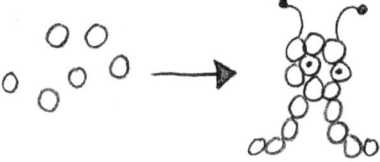

Imagine when the first separate, free-living cells on our planet conjoined. Cells working together opened immense horizons, including the possibility of *you*. All of a sudden, new ways of moving, eating, and reproducing became possible. Without that ancient AND, we would never have had the potential for bodies, eyes, cucumbers, and guinea pigs.

AND is a possibility creator.

In contrast,

OR is a possibility destroyer.

Wouldn't you rather live in a world with humans AND chimpanzees (instead of us OR them)? Aren't you glad to have eyes AND ears, land AND sky, sun AND moon, fire AND water? Imagine how many fewer possibilities would exist if you had to choose between the elements.

Of course, there are times when nature splits things apart. And there are times in our lives to say no, close a door, or make a decisive choice. OR is a great word. It just shouldn't run your life.

When we live an OR life, we limit and constrain ourselves. When we live an AND life, we step out of conflict and into our true creativity.

Getting Out of the Box

AND does far more than allow us to write complex sentences. AND helps us live full, joyful, and creative lives.

AND wants you to get out of the box and into your life.

In the first chapter, I asked you to give up lines. To give up the false promise of a linear life. I also asked you to consider saying goodbye to boxes. You don't need to fit in a box, and neither does your life.

These days, we live mostly in square houses and sleep in square rooms and work at square desks and wear relatively square clothes.

We're surrounded by pressures to conform. Sure, it's easier to build a square house and easier to live a square life. But is that really what you want?

I know you might be thinking, *"Easier said than done."* Never fear. I'll give you a process for getting out of the box.

You also might be thinking, *"That's a lot to give up."* Just consider that if you give up straight lines and confining boxes, what's left is basically everything else in the universe. You can connect the threads of your life into any shape you want.

By the way, AND loves unusual shapes. It loves you how you actually are. It doesn't call you a square peg in a round hole. It asks if you might like to try on an amoeba shape—or, perchance, add some sparkly sneakers for your pseudopods.

AND has no predefined opinion about who you are, who you should be, or how your life might take shape. In fact, AND doesn't like the word "*should*" at all.

AND would love to see you soar. AND would also love to see others soar. There's nothing mutually exclusive about it.

AND operates from a mentality of generous possibility, not stingy scarcity.

A life lived with AND is chock-full of:

· Creativity
· Courage
· Connection
· Clarity
· Compassion
· Curiosity
· Confidence
· Capacity
· Celebration

When we tap into AND-thinking, we are creative leaders, open-hearted lovers, and engaged community members.

We're also great at seeing the big picture. We're no longer pouting about our lives and trying to separate pleasure from pain. We're no longer seeing impossible tradeoffs between parts of our personality, facets of our family, or sectors of society. *We understand the whole.* Remember, AND is all about the 100 Percent Club.

AND is constantly offering creative possibilities for our lives. The problem is that we aren't always listening. When we are stuck in old ways of thinking and living, it's hard to imagine what a new way would look like in our lives.

In the next chapter, I'll walk you through a specific process for fostering AND in your life. But even without a formal method, we can still say yes to AND if we are paying attention.

Let's zip back to a time when I was only just beginning to hear the whisper of AND, and I made a decision that would change my life.

A Round House

Just before the pandemic, I was on sabbatical in a tiny town in Colorado. I was taking a semester away from UC Berkeley to work on new projects and offer my kids a new experience.

It was a great change of pace—a single traffic light in the entire county, a lone paved road in town, and endless wilderness to explore. Foxes would come poking around the back door, and bears would occasionally lounge in the front yard apple tree. A far cry from life in Berkeley.

A month into our time in Colorado, the Bay Area went on lockdown, California schools went online, and there was no reason to return immediately to Berkeley. I was teaching online so my son and daughter could temporarily stay in their small, rural Colorado school.

Our six-month sabbatical kept extending until it seemed like we had accidentally moved to Colorado. When the Bay Area opened up again, my kids were settled in their new lives. I was the only one with any reason to return.

In an OR world, this would have been untenable. I would have needed to choose between my job and my family. But with the rumblings of AND in my life, it seemed great to get creative. I started commuting across state lines. I would go to California to teach, Colorado to parent, and various other places to consult and facilitate workshops.

In any other phase of my life, this would have drained my last iota of energy. But all of a sudden, it seemed energizing and fun.

That spring, when I was in Berkeley, spending time with my students and wrapping up the semester, I got sick. It wasn't anything serious, but it had me laid up in bed for a few days. One afternoon, I was flopped sideways across the bed with a high fever. As I drifted in and out of sleep, my feverish thoughts roamed.

And then, seemingly out of nowhere, I thought, "*round house, New Mexico.*" The sentence fragment was light like a feather. It wasn't a brick—or a soccer goal—but

it had *energy*. And I'd reached a place where I no longer needed to be hit in the head to pay attention.

I squirmed myself to the edge of the bed where I could
reach my laptop, went to a house-hunting site, and typed
"*round house, New Mexico*" into the search bar.

Why did I reach for my computer? Why did I go to a
house-hunting site? I have no idea. I wasn't in the market
for a new home and certainly wasn't looking to move across
the country (again). But I had started believing that Life
was working a lot of magic behind the scenes, and it was
my job to listen.

Plus, "*round house, New Mexico*" wasn't just a literal possibility; it was a deeper invitation.

I had been in Berkeley on and off for more than twenty
years, but it still wasn't *my place*. In contrast, New Mexico
had always inexplicably felt like *home*.

I grew up in Brooklyn, but my family would occasionally
drive to national parks in the summer. Once, when I was
about nine, we drove through New Mexico. I remember crossing the Rio Grande and feeling an incredible
longing to stay. Later, when I became a biologist, I spent
long months alone in New Mexico, studying lizards and
desert ecology.

So, hearing *New Mexico* in my feverish state wasn't just
about the physical place. It was about opening an inquiry
into the idea of *home*. My new rhythm had largely resolved

the tension in my life between career and family. But it was just the beginning. I hadn't yet found a place where my love of solitude and nature could flourish. I needed to expand the AND.

Similarly, *round house* wasn't just about an architectural structure. It was about stepping out of the box. I had begun to craft a creative life, but I was still operating within very constrained and ossified structures. I was increasingly tired of the traditional university system but couldn't yet picture a new direction for my career.

So, I typed *"round house, New Mexico,"* and the listing on top stopped me in my tracks. It was indeed a round house. It was in Taos, New Mexico, right next to the Rio Grande. I was flooded with longing and a feeling of being at home.

My mind kicked back on and yelled, *"Hello!?! You have a job in California and a family in Colorado. There is absolutely no way you can entertain this! You can't afford to buy a new house! You can't take any more time away from the kids! You can't throw away your career for some stupid dream!"*

It was an OR tirade. I knew that voice, full of judgment and scarcity and fear. But I had also started listening for the quiet call of AND.

AND has a subtle confidence, like the universe is offering you an invitation with a wink. AND smiles and encourages you to do something wonderful while OR carries on with a one-sided screaming match.

That afternoon, AND didn't say, *"Throw caution to the wind! Quit your job! Leave your kids! Become a desert hermit!"* AND simply said, *"Round house, New Mexico. Want me to start generating possibilities?"*

AND is happy to offer small steps toward big transformation.

The house that popped up on that search changed my life—but not in a linear way. After all, how could a round house have linear effects?

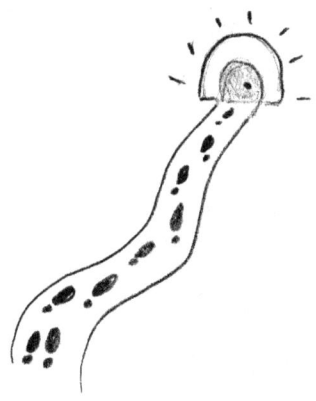

I'll tell you more about that round house as we continue along. For now, just know that it changed me in ways I never could have imagined. Once you start saying yes to AND, the possibilities are endless.

The Reality of AND

AND helps us get out of the box and try on new shapes.

You don't need to know ahead of time where you're going. You don't need to say, *"I'd like to stop feeling so confined. I want a life that looks like a circle or snail shell or dodecahedron."* Instead, a simple *"I'd like to stop feeling so boxed in"* is enough to kickstart the process.

Sure, every once in a while, you'll get a specific direction like *"round house, New Mexico."* But more typically, you'll just be living and listening and not worrying too much about the shape of your life. It will be a delightful shape because it will be *yours.*

If you're ready to get real about how to cultivate an AND life, great. I'll give you a specific process in the next section of the book.

And if you're still on the fence, let yourself be on the fence. AND doesn't mind.

Feel free to jot down some of your fears or reservations about living an AND life. Maybe it sounds like a big change. Or maybe you're afraid you'll rock the boat in your current situation. Or maybe you've been disappointed by the promise of change before. No problem.

AND lives in the moment. It works with you, starting where you actually are. It creates unexpected connections, unusual combinations, and courageous possibilities.

AND is ready to get to know you better.

After all, the introductory party is over. OR is trying to get you to put your heavy coat back on (while slipping more rocks into the pockets). AND is walking out the door into the beautiful night, asking if you want to keep in touch. If I were you, I'd give AND your number.

&

PART II

Living AND

CHAPTER 4

The OR-to-cAND Framework

More Small Words

Life is full of enormous questions.

And yet, the words that lead us into even our most life-changing explorations are tiny.

As you know, this book is inspired by two small conjunctions: AND plus OR. Now it's time to chat with their little grammatical friends, the interrogative adverbs and pronouns. Let's get clear about what we'll be doing together by answering their questions.

What: The *what* is simple. Our quest is to shift our thinking and living from OR to AND.

Why: Your *why* should also now feel palpable. OR lives are constrained, conflicted, and compartmentalized.

OR leaves us feeling dissatisfied and diminished. In contrast, AND lives are creative, courageous, and celebratory. AND inspires a sense of expansive possibility and authentic joy.

Feel free to jot down anything else you've noticed about your personal *why*. Even a single sentence written in your own words will help clarify and personalize your motivation.

Who: The *who* is important. I wrote this book for you. Even if we have never met, you're the one person I had in mind when I wrote this sentence. Really? Yes.

Whenever I work with large groups, I design my programs to offer maximum value for all participants. That said, the only way to offer value to many is to make it personal for each. So, I always imagine that there is *one person* in the audience with whom it's critical for me to connect.

I don't pray that *everyone* will love me. I just hope that my presence will matter to one person. The beautiful thing is that there can be many "one persons." Then magical things happen.

Even when I'm giving a more formal talk, things pop into my mind that I don't understand but simply need to say. After the event, someone always comes up to share how that sentence felt like it was spoken directly to them.

The same is true with writing. I'm not writing in a vacuum. I'm sensing you out there, somewhere, reading. This book has 40,868 words. It's quite likely that some of them were written specifically for you.

Where and When: I'm a big fan of the *here and now*. It requires no additional preparation or planning and allows you to be exactly as you are right now.

Technically, if you think about it, it's also the only option. Go ahead; just try to do something outside of the here and now. And then come on back, and let's get rolling.

How: Any journey of personal transformation needs a *how*—processes and practices to support and inspire you.

In my coaching and consulting work, I weave together personal reflection, group activities, guided meditation, and art exploration to help people shift from OR to AND. In this book, I've distilled my OR-to-AND approach into a series of self-guided activities you can apply to your life right now.

Next, I'll flesh out the OR-to-AND framework. Then, I'll introduce a powerful process to transform OR to AND, plus offer a series of exercises to deepen the journey.

But first, let me invite you to join my not-so-secret club.

The AND-ers

When I started as a young biology professor in 2008, I always looked forward to receiving my teaching evaluations at the end of the semester. In my first few years, I taught a big introductory biology class in an old lecture hall—students arrayed in wooden auditorium seats, learning about the peculiarities of life on Earth:

- Peacock spiders have amazing courtship dances.
- Some lizards can shoot blood out of their eyes to deter predators.
- Sharks are fish, even though you probably think they aren't.

I was an enthusiastic instructor, and my end-of-semester reviews were typically positive. Well, except for the student who said, "*You should dress nicer.*" (noted) and "*You should curse less.*" (duly noted).

But in those early years, I was sharing facts about science, not questions about life. So, my course reviews said things like, "*This course inspired me to love biology,*" but not "*This course inspired me to love life.*"

Shortly after I got hit in the head, something curious started happening at the end of the semester. Students began lobbying for my courses to continue.

Normally, at the end of the term, students fly off campus. It's like the iconic scene in the movies, where the bell rings and the students burst out of heavy doors, papers flying, freedom calling.

But now, students were waiting for me in the hallway after the last class, asking what we could do next together. And the interesting thing was they knew what they wanted:

"We know you're teaching us biology. But there's something else you really care about. What if you offered us a class about that?"

Here's the thing. I had been discouraged from becoming a teacher my whole life. I'd been weaned on the old adage: *Those who can, do. Those who can't, teach.* That was compounded by my mother—a beleaguered teacher in the New York City public schools—offering a regular refrain of *"Do anything you want; just don't become a teacher."*

But I was irrevocably drawn to teaching. Put me at a party with an amazing cocktail in my hand, and I'll shrink down to the size of a peanut. But put me in a classroom with an old dusty stump of chalk in my hand, and I come alive.

The *context* of teaching was always so thrilling for me. The *content* almost didn't matter. But now my students were asking for more. And they were right. I had only been teaching half of what I knew about biology.

Biology is the study of life. Most textbooks will make learning biology feel like eating stale beef jerky. But life— *LIFE*—is the most interesting thing in the universe. Studying life isn't just about memorizing the Krebs cycle. It's about being curious about *everything*. From microbes to mammals, brains to biopsies, cells to consciousness.

Being interested in life is not just a narrow intellectual pursuit. It's not about the dispassionate study of something "out there." It's also about understanding what's happening "in here" in our own bodies, minds, and lives.

The mistake I made for the first ten years of my career was that I had been teaching the *facts* of biology without exposing the *heart* of a person fascinated by life itself. Getting hit on the head shattered the separation between "out there" and "in here," and more of my love of life was pouring into my teaching. Even so, my students were asking for more, and I started dreaming of how to rise to the occasion.

A few weeks later, I was sitting at the scratched wooden table in the office of my department chair, letting my fingers run along the imperfections in the grain while proposing my first "weird" class, where my students would study themselves and the planet at the same time. I was terrified that I'd be fired.

Instead, my department chair was thrilled. He leaned in and said conspiratorially, *"It's wonderful that you want to do this. Our students need help with their personal growth, and most of our faculty have no idea where to start."*

So, I began offering classes that I actually wanted to teach. Now, my end-of-semester evaluations started saying, *"This course changed my life."* But the same thing happened at the end of the term—students hung back in the classroom, wishing the course wouldn't end and wanting me to offer classes that others in their lives could attend.

So, my teaching started spilling out of the classroom and out of the university. I had accidentally started a coaching and consulting business. As the years went on, I would offer courses and workshops to students and leaders around the world. But that first year, it was a small group sitting on the floor of my living room every other Thursday, drinking tea out of wobbly mugs and eating mid-brow chocolate bars.

It was immensely liberating. My teaching no longer needed to fit into any particular degree requirements, any specific discipline, or any fixed number of semester weeks. I was free to discover what worked best to support deep transformation without predetermined constraints.

I had spent years studying and practicing in many different modalities but had always kept them separate. I taught science to scientists, meditation to meditators, bodywork to bodyworkers, and art to artists. Now, I could bring the most effective transformative practices together under one roof.

The result was powerful. Every one of those original group members stepped into a life of great possibility. They developed faith in themselves, fellowship with each other, and more freedom in their lives. Even once the group stopped meeting formally, the connection and transformation continued to deepen. The original group members are still the ones who show up for each other to celebrate new horizons and console deep losses. They are the ones who lean in and whisper, "*AND*?" when it's time to go deeper or cry harder or dream bigger.

Every group eventually has a name. The best names are those that appear spontaneously, without pretense or analysis. That first group went through several iterations before we spontaneously started calling ourselves the AND-ers.

The AND-ers approach isn't something I sat down and tried to develop strategically. It's something that emerged from decades of *seeing what inspires lasting transformation in people's lives.*

In all of the ways I work with people—from one-on-one coaching to small group retreats to conference workshops to large stages—AND has shown me over and over again that it knows how to change lives.

So, consider this an invitation to join our secret club. Even if you're not sitting in my living room eating chocolate bars, you're still an AND-er.

Let's look at how to bring AND into *your* living room—and anywhere else you travel.

Change Your Mind

I told you in the first chapter that one of my favorite sentences of all time is, "*I changed my mind.*"

Being able to change your mind comes in handy for daily life. You can change your mind about your favorite ice cream flavor, a particular commitment at work, the best approach for staying healthy, or the place of a certain relationship in your life.

The arc of your life is actually defined by all the ways you have changed your mind. You may have shifted your perspective about where to live, how to work, who to befriend, or what to eat. Those changes led to other changes, which eventually led you to this moment.

Sure, your path has also been influenced by forces beyond your control. But if you look closely, you'll see that the power of external factors lies largely in how they change *you*. Real transformation comes when you change your mind.

What's interesting is that the connection between your thoughts and your choices is also evident in the small decisions you make in your daily life.

Before I popped open my computer to search for a desert abode, I thought, "*round house, New Mexico.*"

Before I get up for a cup of water, I think, "*I'm thirsty.*"

And before I tuck the dogs in the bedroom and greet the lovely lady who fills my water cistern when we don't get enough rain, I think, "*I need to keep the dogs inside so they don't bark at April.*"

You might not always see or hear the thought in bold font in your mind. You might not even know where the thought came from. But if you look closely, you'll find that thought precedes action.

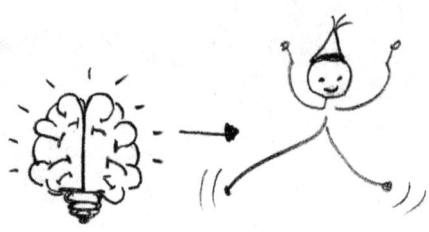

You may see where I'm going here.

Our thinking informs our living. So, if you want to change the circumstances of your life, you need to change your mind first.

If you're living an Oʀ life, you can't just swap it for an Aɴᴅ life. You first need to transform your thinking.

The connection between your thinking and your living is fundamental to the Oʀ-to-Aɴᴅ framework.

Playground Games

Permit me a short detour. Did you play foursquare as a kid?

If so, conjure up that big round playground ball and your competitive spirit. If not, I suggest you grab some friends and sidewalk chalk and give it a whirl (maybe finish this chapter first).

Foursquare is a game with, well, four squares... drawn on the ground, something like this:

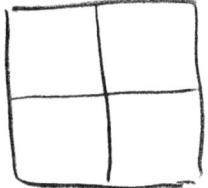

One player stands in each square, and players spike a big ball around the squares, trying to force each other "out" by missing the ball. The "best" square is A-square, and the "worst" square is D-square. The goal is to advance to A-square. When a player gets out, they're bumped back to D-square.

Now, here's what's interesting about our analogy. There's only one route you can take through the squares. You always start at D-square, and as other players get out, you progress by moving one square to your right toward A-square. You can't jump from D to A, even if you're the one who made the amazing play. You've got to progress in a set order.

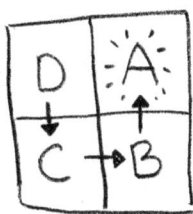

If you get to A-square, you stay there as long as you can. And when you do get out—which you eventually will— you start over at D-square. You don't walk back through each square one by one. You swallow your pride and start again at the bottom.

Great, now that you know the rules, let's play a little four-square with your life.

Making ᴀND from Oʀ

Why did I take you back to your elementary school playground? Because I think it will help you remember our Oʀ-to-ᴀND approach.

Let's look at our process for transforming constraint to creativity in a simple foursquare.

We've got the Oʀ way (the old way) and the ᴀND way (the new way). We also have our patterns of thought (the causes), which influence the circumstances of our lives (the consequences). So, there are four squares: Oʀ-living, which comes from Oʀ-thinking, and ᴀND-living, which comes from ᴀND-thinking.

Now, let's go wild with the foursquare analogy. We've got an analog for D-square: the Oʀ life (your starting place). And an analog for A-square: the ᴀND life (your goal). And we have a set path to travel through the squares.

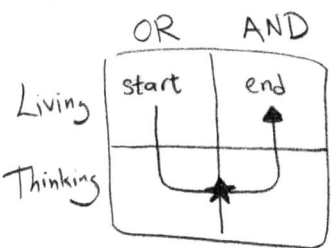

We start where we are—OR-living. Note that this is not a negative judgment about our lives. It's a call to action. Even if you are thrilled with 99 percent of your life, you can still use this framework to explore the 1 percent that's feeling constrained. And let's be honest, I'm guessing we've all got a little more than 1 percent to play with.

A lot of spiritual and self-help traditions jump straight into working with the mind, but I like to start with what's easiest to see—the circumstances of our lives. Remember, the evidence of your thinking is on display in the conditions, conflicts, and constraints of your life.

Once we see our patterns of OR-living clearly, we can find our underlying habits of OR-thinking. This is simultaneously horrifying and empowering. It's painful to realize that you've been a prisoner... to yourself.

However, it's also deeply empowering to recognize that you hold the keys to change. If you can create an OR life from your thoughts, then you also have the power to create an AND life with a simple change of mind.

So, here's the point of true transformation: the *internal* moment we shift from OR to AND.

When we aren't happy with the circumstances of our lives, we often try to change the *externals* without addressing the *internals*. But the master key for all lasting transformation is the *inner shift*.

Once we've made that inner shift, the external changes we desire *emerge* from our change of mind. I'm not saying it's easy to redesign your life, but now you'll be working in concert with yourself. You can try to change your external circumstances in a million different ways, but if you don't address your limiting beliefs, you'll always end up back in D-square.

Your Way

Foursquare is an *analogy*. In real life, you're not trying to advance squares. You are *living*—and life doesn't like boxes or straight lines. Plan to meander and see some sights. Everything you learn about the territory of your mind will pay dividends the next time it feels like you're booted back to the beginning.

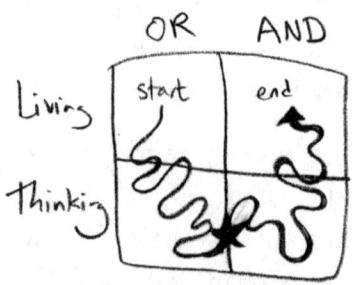

Changing your thinking from OR to AND is not a pres-to-chango, one-and-done situation. In reality, your path from D-square to A-square may be a little wiggly. You may dredge up some old demons. You may teeter on the edge of change. You may have OR relapses. In the coming chapters, I'll offer specific guidance on how to work with the squiggly road.

For now, please don't get fixated on staying in A-square. It doesn't matter how often you make it to AND-land, and it doesn't matter how long your reign lasts. Any small taste of AND just primes the pump for your next adventure. No matter how unreasonably smart and talented you are, sometimes you get out. The ball whizzes by before you even know what happened. Have some humility and get back in the game. D-square can be your friend once you know how to move past it.

Also, you don't need to compete with anyone, including yourself. You get to take this journey in your own time and way. No one has to get home before dark. No one will lose if you win. No one needs to enforce the rules. And sure, you can go to the playground if that floats your boat, but you can transform OR to AND anytime, anyplace.

So, play the game *your way*. Put on some sneakers, and let's get to it.

CHAPTER 5

The OR-to-AND Process

Four Squares and Four Questions

Remember our framework for moving around the OR-to-AND foursquare?

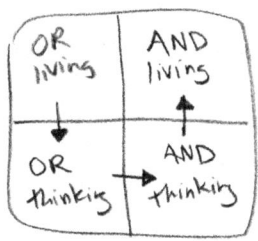

When we find ourselves in OR-living, we want to expose our underlying OR-thinking. Once we expose OR-thinking, we can change our minds to foster AND-thinking. And when we are open to AND-thinking, we have unfathomable opportunities for AND-living.

At this point, you might be wondering, "*HOW* are we going to do this?"

In this chapter, I'll give you a powerful Oʀ-to-Aɴᴅ process to transform constraint into creativity.

Let's translate our foursquare into a set of four simple and universal questions carefully designed to guide you through the Oʀ-to-Aɴᴅ journey. The questions map onto our foursquare like this:

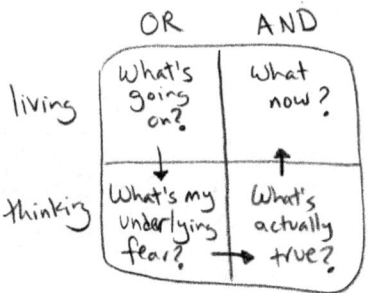

The four questions form a path that can bring you into conversation with your life at any time or in any place or circumstance.

Let's look at why these particular questions are so powerful and how to engage with them.

Asking the Four Questions

Let's meet the four questions before we practice applying them to situations in our lives.

Anytime we notice we are in D-square with OR-living, we can simply ask:

1. *What's going on?*

In other words, what feels challenging, conflicted, or constraining in your life?

Notice that the first question always starts right where you are—with the circumstances of your life. Typically, you won't need to go looking for conflict. It will find you.

It's important to remember that challenge is a natural and important part of our lives. Just because you encounter a challenge doesn't mean you did something wrong. It also doesn't mean the world did something wrong to you.

It's easy to get stuck in D-square if you see yourself as a villain or a victim. Your goal isn't to eliminate discomfort from your life (that would be impossible). Your quest is to engage meaningfully with adversity to foster a life of greater possibility.

So, the goal of the first question is to provide a quick snapshot of the issue at hand. Don't get stuck in a long story; just distill the situation to its essence.

Once you have identified something that feels painful or tight in your life, it's time to move to C-square. We can reveal our OR-thinking by asking:

2. *What's my underlying fear?*

In other words, what limiting thoughts and beliefs underlie your situation?

The second question peels back the curtain to reveal OR-thinking.

Thoughts that create OR-living are powered by fear. They tell you that you are limited, broken, or unworthy. We have to see these thoughts clearly before we can break their spell.

You can't move past C-square unless you listen to your inner dialogue with receptivity, not judgment. Usually, there's a lot of material in C-square. Be patient and let old fears bubble up.

Once you have a sense of your captivatingly constraining thoughts, you're ready for the big shift to B-square. We can seed the transformation to AND-thinking with the question:

3. What's actually true?

The third question cuts right to the heart of the matter. We can believe all kinds of lies and feed all sorts of distortions. In the end, we need to ask what is actually true.

Shifting from OR-thinking to AND-thinking is simple but not easy. This question is impossible to answer from the head; we have to move down to the heart.

If you try to engage with the third question from OR-thinking, you will fail. OR will just say, "*Those things ARE true. You are stuck. You do have to make a difficult choice and live in a crappy world.*" However, the moment you stop listening to OR, a private and receptive space emerges.

That still space will usually offer quiet, instantaneous answers. Don't miss them. The answers that emerge bring us to A-square. We transform AND-thinking to AND-living by asking:

4. What now?

In other words, what's possible if you believe in—and act from—your deeper capacity and creativity?

Now that you're in a receptive mood, the fourth question helps you make the shift from possibility to action.

We don't actually need to resolve all of our internal tensions and limitations before living an AND life. Sometimes, it's enough to *imagine* the choice we might make—or the life we might lead—if we believed in expansive possibility.

The answer to the fourth question is often unexpected and helps you see the bigger picture. Once you see it, you are free to make any choice. You are free to move forward in a new way. You are also free to stay in your current situation. AND doesn't make any demands. AND just wants you to know you have incredible options.

And many of these options would have stayed hidden if you hadn't gone through the full foursquare process.

Let's look at this process in action.

Pears, Fears, and Babies

When I was a young graduate student pursuing my PhD, I went to a phenomenally depressing lecture in UC Berkeley's enormous Zellerbach Hall. The lecture was given by a leading family law scholar and was about the probability of career success in academia.

I'm sure the lecture ended with an inspiring call to action, but all I remember was the analogy illustrating the vanishingly small probability of career advancement for women. The speaker said, *"Men are like apples, and women are like pears. If you look at the bottom (in entry-level positions), an apple and a pear look roughly the same. But as you go up (to leadership positions), apples get wider, and pears get narrower."*

Her point was a statistical reality. The probability of long-term career advancement for women in academia was dramatically lower than for men. And for women with children, the odds were even worse.

The tension between family and career may seem like a well-worn topic, but it remains an arena where OR often holds sway. It's a pervasive concern for many of my students and clients, and it was a pressing apprehension for me as I listened to that lecture. I was about to finish my PhD and wanted to start a family.

Fast forward a few years to 2008. My daughter was one year old, and I had just started my first faculty position at the University of Idaho. I was invited back to UC Berkeley to give a lecture celebrating 100 years of science at the university. The lecture hall wasn't quite as big as Zellerbach, but it felt like a huge honor to be asked to discuss the future of science at a centennial celebration.

At the reception after my talk, a respected senior colleague cornered me. He didn't want to talk about the science I had just presented. He just wanted to give me this advice:

"Bree, it looks like your career is going great. Just don't have another baby. That will really ruin things for you."

I don't remember how I responded to my colleague at that moment. All I remember is the sinking feeling.

I was accustomed to being questioned about my personal and professional choices, but this was a direct assault by Or. It was also one I would hear again and again throughout my early career.

I'm fairly driven and independent by nature. After the lecture in Zellerbach Hall, I decided to proceed as if the statistics didn't apply to me. After the encounter at the centennial celebration, I tried to pretend my colleague's words didn't rankle.

But there was always a background tension in my mind and in my life: *Maybe everyone's right. Maybe career and family are at odds. Maybe I'm a pear after all.*

Answering the Four Questions

Let's practice working with the four questions using my centennial celebration experience as an example.

That day in the lecture hall, when my colleague told me not to have another child, it activated a *pre-existing inner conflict.* If I hadn't already felt tension between my family and my career, I simply wouldn't have cared about his opinion. The fact that his comment got under my skin was because I already felt stressed and torn about navigating these arenas of my life.

Here's the unscripted conversation I just had with my young 2008 self.

1. *What's going on?*

   I feel so much tension between my personal and professional desires.

2. *What's my underlying fear?*

   I can't do both.

   My time and energy are limited.

   Society isn't set up for me to succeed.

I don't have the support I need.

I have to play by other people's rules.

3. What's actually true?

I want BOTH a fulfilling family life and a vibrant vocation.

It's MY job to find my own path.

It's an honor—not a burden—to do things my own way.

I don't need to know ahead of time how it's all going to work out.

It doesn't matter if academic culture is set up for me to thrive.

I have a greater reservoir of support than I can possibly fathom.

4. What now?

Pursue all of my passions simultaneously.

Don't cut off any of my own arms—they might come in handy later.

Create my own support networks; don't rely on what already exists.

Think bigger and do my job differently.

Support others who are struggling to break free.

That exploration took me just a few minutes, and there's a lot of gold there. Sure, some of the entries may seem cheesy or abstract, but each one is actionable. Now, nearly two decades later, I can see *exactly* how those AND possibilities could have created a road map for fulfillment and joy.

But at the time, I hadn't developed my AND-not-OR process. So, instead of using that moment of challenge for self-inquiry, I let my colleague's judgment feed a negative belief system and increase the tension in my life. So many answers were waiting for me at the time, but I didn't know how to access them.

I had to wait another five years before the pressure built so high that Life decided to hit me in the head with a soccer goal.

Luckily, you don't need to wait another moment.

It's your turn. Pick something that feels like a conflict you'd like to explore. Don't overthink it; just pick the first thing that comes to mind. If multiple situations are vying for your attention, keep a list and come back to this process as often as you like. The door is always open.

The first few times you engage with the process, it might feel clunky. Be patient. It takes time to get the *feel* of AND. In the coming chapters, I'll give you lots of ways to build your confidence in the process. For now, just give it a whirl.

Going Deeper with the Four Questions

Before we wrap up this chapter, I want to give you some additional pointers and examples of working with the OR-to-AND questions.

There are two main ways to engage with the four questions:

First, you can work with the questions as a form of *general reflection*. In the morning, you can zip around the four-square to set the mood for your day. In the evening, you can reflect on anything that feels unresolved from your day. Anytime you like, you can zoom out and explore a more general or persistent conflict in your life.

Second, you can also work with the questions as a form of *specific inquiry*. In this case, you can call the questions up in real time whenever you feel yourself slipping into an OR mentality. Perhaps you had an altercation with a new lover or a run-in with an old demon. Maybe you're nervous about an upcoming meeting or woke up feeling off. Anytime OR is in the room, you'll tighten up— mentally, emotionally, or physically. When you notice a feeling of constriction in real time, the four questions can be a guide and a support.

We are deeply habituated to either avoid or indulge negative feelings. We bypass or brood. Instead, we can engage directly with our challenges and learn from the moment-to-moment experiences of our lives.

When your OR radar goes off, simply pause and ask yourself the first question: *What's going on?*

Don't launch into a novella about your circumstances. Don't worry if the situation sounds trivial or lofty. Just articulate the situation to yourself in a single sentence without filters. Some examples from students and clients:

· I'm nervous about the board meeting this afternoon.
· I'm feeling betrayed by my partner.
· I don't know which cancer treatment is right for me.
· I'm feeling an enormous wave of grief.
· I don't know what color to paint the living room.

Your job is simply to listen and record your thoughts and fears. It doesn't matter if they seem big or small, profound or mundane. You don't need to analyze them or explore their history. Simply acknowledge them and move on.

Then, go to the second question: *What's my underlying fear?*

Don't hold back, and don't edit. Listen for at least three to five possible fears. Yours may be unique each time you engage with the process, or you may notice running themes. For example:

- I'm afraid they won't like me.
- I'm afraid I don't have what it takes to succeed.
- I'm afraid I can't handle what's coming next.
- I'm afraid I'll feel like this forever.
- I'm afraid I'm irrevocably broken.

You are revealing deep and important fears to yourself. Don't rush. Act like a dear friend to yourself. Listen. Acknowledge. Feel.

When you're ready, move on to the third question and ask: *What's actually true?*

Get yourself in the AND mood. Take a deep breath and listen for any quiet truth that bubbles up. This is not a time for your logical mind to go into overdrive trying to make you feel better. This is a time to listen for unexpected invitations. The truth won't be a one-for-one rebuttal of your fears, but it's often related.

If you feel stuck, just gently repeat one of your fears to yourself. For example, imagine that you're anxious about a big upcoming meeting and you're working with the fear *"I'm afraid they won't like me."* If you listen with an open heart, you might hear:

- It's true that they might not like me.
- I'm ready to be stretched.
- Your capacity is far greater than you know.
- Whose love matters most?
- There's a bigger picture that you don't yet see.

Some answers might be in the first person, others in the third. Some might be questions, and others may be statements. It doesn't matter. Write what you hear. Even if the examples above mean nothing to you, I guarantee that the truths that emerge from *your process* will.

Finally, stay in the AND mood and ask the fourth question: *What now?*

If you were working with fear about an upcoming work event, you might hear:

· Prepare for the meeting as if they already love you.
· Imagine yourself standing in front of the room with a wide smile and open arms.
· Show your humanity.
· Change the seating arrangement into a circle.
· Get up and go for a walk right now.

Trust what you hear and *act on it*. OR wants to keep you paralyzed with fear. AND wants to help you move forward. Take one small and simple action that honors what you heard. Even if you don't take immediate action, don't reject the answers to the fourth question as fanciful or unrealistic. Otherwise, you'll be back in D-square, feeding OR again.

And if you do find yourself spun up or spun out, it's no problem. Every time you engage with the questions, you learn about yourself. You can always come back and play foursquare another time.

Personal and Universal

One of the things that I love about the four questions is that they are simultaneously personal and universal.

The OR-to-AND process is there for everyone, and the questions are crafted to work with universal principles of transformation.

Also, the questions stay the same each time. They are a doorway that's easy to find. Even when you feel lost or scared, the questions are there. You can open the door at any time, in any place, and for any situation in your life.

always here

Once you ask the questions, you enter a landscape that's quite personal and ever-changing. The doorway stays the same. The territory beyond is a unique playground for *you* at *this* moment.

Engaging with the questions is a way of exploring your inner territory with a trustworthy compass. Each time you ask the questions, you will enter a vast and fascinating landscape. Your job is to simply stay curious about what you find.

In my experience living and teaching transformation, I've found that any effective and enduring approach to personal transformation needs two things:

- Something simple you can remember
- Something deep you can discover

So far, I've shared with you a framework (the foursquare) and a process (the four questions), which will guide you on a journey of discovery. Just returning to the questions, again and again, will precipitate great shifts toward freedom and joy in your life.

And yet, I want to offer you a more complete—and personalized—system for working with Oʀ and Aɴᴅ in all arenas of your life. So, let's turn to the practices I've developed to support your Oʀ-to-Aɴᴅ journey.

CHAPTER 6

The OR-to-AND Practices

Authentic Inquiry

Every effective transformational approach balances simplicity and depth. Also, every robust transformational approach has a framework, a process, and a living body of supporting practices.

A potent framework takes a fundamental aspect of human experience and makes it tangible. The simplest framework for our work together is OR-to-AND. It's easy to remember and will serve as a touchstone as you shift from constraint to creativity.

OR-to-AND describes our big-picture journey, but it doesn't capture an essential truth about transformation—our thoughts shape our lives. Thus, we have our foursquare to remind us that OR-thinking leads to OR-living, and AND-thinking leads to AND-living.

Is there really a stark dividing line between our inner thoughts and our outer lives? Can you show me exactly where your thoughts end and your life begins?

Of course not. That's why it's a *framework*. A framework is a *way of understanding reality*. It isn't reality itself. You can't eat a framework for breakfast or drive a framework to work. You can't knit a sweater for your framework or crawl into your framework's loving arms when you're utterly spent.

Sure, we want our OR-to-AND framework to map something essential and meaningful, but the framework itself is still a *concept,* a way of understanding.

What defines the value of a framework is not only how close it comes to mapping the truth of our experience but also whether it's *useful.* A framework should be able to prove its worth by *working well in our lives.*

The way a framework comes alive—and works in our lives—is through the *process* it inspires.

In our case, our foursquare framework gives rise to our four questions. Not only does each question map to a specific part of the framework, but the questions offer a *specific path* through the transformational process. You can't eat the process for breakfast either, but you can see its tangible effects on your life.

A framework might change the way you think, but a process changes your life.

So, even if the book ended here, you would have a framework and a process that you could explore for years to come.

And yet, the book doesn't end here. Because for me, there is one more essential dimension to successful transformation.

We need a framework (check), a process inspired by that framework (check), and a living body of supportive practices. Practice is what takes us deeper into our transformation. Practice is what provides inspiration and confidence on our path. Practice is what helps us see our blind spots and overcome our obstacles.

The OR-to-AND practices are all centered around *inquiry*. This is intentional. Inquiry, reflection, and contemplation are common elements in all transformative practices—from meditation to prayer to therapy to art.

I've developed the OR-to-AND practices drawing from decades of study and practice in these different modalities. The strategies I'll share are simply the most meaningful and effective, both in my own life and for the people and organizations I work with. Now you can make them yours.

The OR-to-AND practices don't have a *my-way-or-the-highway* vibe. Instead, they say *cuddle-me-up-in-your-life-as-it-is*. You still can't eat them for breakfast, but maybe you can knit them a sweater or let them join you on your drive to work.

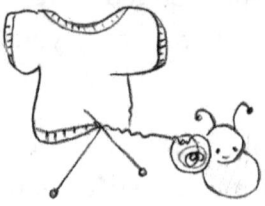

The Scorching Bath

Let's return to the time years ago when I signed up for the Multidimensional Body course after getting hit on the head.

The class met every Thursday night in the same quietly lit chiropractor's office. The sessions were taught jointly by my friend, the Chiropractor, and his friend, the Reverend (which is, itself, a lesson in AND). At the end of each session, we'd sit in a circle on the floor, and the Doc and the Rev would give us homework for the week.

This particular week, the homework had three steps:

1. *Make a list of everyone you have ever wronged or felt wronged by.*
2. *Conduct a short ceremony to release the bonds of guilt and blame.*
3. *Take a hot bath.*

I had set aside a small blank journal for course notes and reflections. I like journals with unlined pages and bare covers. It's like the journal doesn't know exactly what to expect from me, so I'm free to roam, free to be inconsistent, incoherent, or a little bit unhinged.

I spent a few days scouring old memories and adding to my list. Then, I set aside an evening when the kids were with their grandma, and I knew I'd have a few hours of uninterrupted time. I sat on my bedroom floor, lit a small candle, propped my journal up, and went down my list one by one.

For each person, I conjured a memory of the time when the shame or blame felt strongest. I sat for a moment with the discomfort of each memory. Then, when I was ready, I said something simple like, *"I release anything I've carried of yours and call back anything you've carried of mine."* Then I paused, felt any energy leaving or returning, wished the person well, and moved on.

After the ritual, I ran a hot bath. Actually, I ran a scalding bath. Somehow, the instructions to *"take a hot bath"* had turned into, *"Take a bath that is as hot as you can possibly stand for as long as you can possibly tolerate."*

If soaking in hot water would somehow help me release guilt and blame, wouldn't a suffer-fest of scalding water work even better?

My Berkeley house had an enormous water heater and an old, deep, enamel, claw-foot tub. I got the water hot enough to be painful and high enough that I could submerge myself completely. I left my nose and mouth out to breathe, and whenever the water started to cool, I added another boiling dose. When I felt completely cooked and more than a little faint, I went to bed.

The next Thursday in class, we shared our experience with the homework. The assignment had cracked open a door into the rich and mysterious Land of Forgiveness. I was starting to understand how shame and blame were stored in my mind and could be released *internally* even years later. It felt revelatory, like I was retrieving parts of myself that I had lost and left behind.

But the feedback I got from Doc and Rev wasn't *"Wow, you did such a good job, sweetie."* It was *"Why on earth did you push yourself to the limit with a **bath**?"* I mean, really, there are lots of ways we humans can push ourselves to the limit. Bathing is not usually one of them.

The magic of the question was that it was genuine, not judgmental. They actually wanted me to find out why I was trying to win a hottest bath competition that didn't even exist.

It was weeks later that I realized the answer to their question was simple: fear and pride.

At that time in my life, I was afraid of not doing it "right," and "it" could be anything—my career, my family, even my meditation practice.

I was also arrogant about my ability to endure difficult things. I was carrying around a subconscious need to prove I could suffer, and it was shutting me down in those same big arenas.

The exercise in forgiveness had quickly turned into a lesson about OR.

I was lugging around an enormous iron either/or scale. I was judging everything—including myself—as right/wrong, strong/weak, worthy/unworthy.

All of a sudden, I could feel the weight—and the cost—of carrying OR.

The reflection prompts from the Multidimensional Body class had brought me into new and unexpected territory. By that point in my life, I had already been meditating for decades. I had spent long months alone in the desert. I had been to therapy. I made art and wrote poetry. But I had always been trying to get somewhere—to clarity, to awakening, to a better version of myself.

I had never simply allowed myself to be *surprised by*—and *interested in*—the dark places inside me. Fear and pride had always seemed like awful traits that I needed to hide or get rid of. Now, they were doorways toward understanding and even forgiveness.

The Scalding Bath Incident taught me the power of *Authentic Inquiry*.

Exercising the Exercises

It's been well over a decade since the Scalding Bath Incident. In that time, my love of inquiry has only deepened. In fact, Authentic Inquiry is the heart of my OR-to-AND process and my work with individuals and organizations around the world.

The four questions are a distilled and powerful form of Authentic Inquiry. No matter how many times you work with the questions, they don't get stale. They keep living and growing with you.

To complement the four questions, I've developed a body of prompts and practices to help you navigate the journey from OR to AND. The next few chapters will give you an introduction to these reflection exercises.

I've designed these exercises to be fast and easy. You'll fill in the blanks and make short lists. You can scribble in the margins of the page, you can get a blank journal of your own, or you can use my dedicated companion journal. The most important thing is simply to *do them*.

Doing the exercises signals something critical to both your conscious and subconscious—that you are ready to learn new things about yourself and your life. Authentic curiosity is a magical thing. Doors will open, and new insights will pour out.

So, here's my top-nine list for *how* to engage with the prompts in the coming pages. Yes, I also thought it should be a top-ten list, but that was OR talking when I heard, "*It's gotta be ten OR it's incomplete.*" So, I'm sticking with nine.

1. **Keep it fast and easy.** You don't need to spend more than five minutes on any of these exercises. Dive deep if you like, but even a quick first pass will pay dividends. Often, if you spend just a few minutes on an exercise, you will have other insights that pop up later in the day without any additional effort.

2. **Trust the first thing.** Write down the first things that pop into your mind, even if they seem strange, scary, or downright ludicrous. Remember, you are trying to sneak past the filters OR uses to constrain you. Get the odd thoughts written down before OR tries to curate you.

3. **Allow contradiction.** Give yourself permission to contradict yourself. You could take the same prompt and answer it in ten wildly different ways. Who says there's one right answer? OR does. Your goal is to blaze past that limitation.

4. **Take multiple passes.** Nothing is too trivial or too deep. Let yourself work with small situations that feel alive *today*. You don't need to go for the hardest, deepest material. You can always come back and trade

your snorkel gear for a SCUBA tank. The prompts are always here for you.

5. **Give yourself some privacy.** Your subconscious will be more forthcoming if it has some privacy. Your insights are for *you*. Don't feel pressure to share them. Which leads me to...

6. **Burn things.** If you're worried about keeping your thoughts private or feel like you need a way to release what you've written, feel free to burn what you write. You'll remember the important insights, and the fire will take care of the rest.

7. **Tolerate (some) discomfort.** Some ORs have been hiding for years, nestled comfortably in the back-reaches of your mind. They may not like having their clothes ripped off. Trust yourself. You'll know when to stay with the discomfort and when to back off. Don't scorch yourself with the exercises in this book. But if you do end up in a scalding bathtub...

8. **Learn from everything.** Everything you learn about yourself matters. Let me repeat that—*everything you learn matters*. Back in the Multidimensional Body class, I thought I was cultivating forgiveness when, really, I was exposing fear and pride. It turned out that the assignment had some bonus homework just for me. Don't get judgy and turn your back on yourself. It's all important.

9. **Do it *your* way.** I suggest you try the exercises the way I wrote them first, but then, feel free to improvise in

whatever way works best for you. This is *your* life and *your* journey. You'll know what you need.

Okay, there's our top nine.

Although, come to think of it, there is one more important thing.

Listening Beyond the Words

The exercises on their own will work wonders, but you'll be doing them without me. I mean, I'm right *here* for you, but I'm not going to be right *there*.

So, I need to teach you a bonus, super-secret advanced skill, which means our list ends up with ten after all:

10. Listen to tone.

Let me explain.

If you were in a coaching session or workshop with me or if I was visiting your organization, I'd know how to guide you to the topics and questions that are most pressing for you. How would I know which ORs are wreaking havoc in your life and which ANDs are waiting to be born? I would know because of the tone of OR's voice and the sound of AND's call.

So, I'd be listening to you (of course). At the same time, I'd be listening for all the subtle ways OR gives itself away and all the quiet ways AND offers an invitation. I'd be listening to the foreground (your words) *and* the background (the energy powering your words).

This may sound esoteric, but it's not. After all, you can feel the energy of anger—or tenderness—in the quality of someone's voice. Tone carries meaning. And you infer this meaning almost instantly, whether you're listening to a lover in your home or overhearing a stranger on the street. We're naturally wired to notice tone.

But you likely have a blind spot. You probably don't usually listen to the tone of *your own* voice or *your own* thoughts. So, I'd like to share some pointers about how to listen for OR and AND in your own life.

At the most basic level, OR has an underlying vibe of negativity, while AND has an underlying energy of positivity. The tricky part is that both have *moods*.

We can arrange the moods of OR and AND on a spectrum from low to high energy. For OR, those moods look like this:

- Vacant
- Numb
- Dull
- Avoidant
- Denying
- Justifying
- Defensive
- Self-Righteous
- Whiny
- Aggressive

A low-energy OR feels vacant and numb, while a high-energy OR feels whiny and aggressive. But regardless of mood, OR *always* has an underlying quality of negativity and self-preservation. OR may shut you down or hype you up, but it always feels exhausting and critical.

Also, OR carries knives. Sometimes, these knives are pointed inward (kindling guilt and shame). Sometimes, these knives are pointed outward (sparking anger and blame).

Even if you don't see the knives, you can *feel* them in the background. The voice of a knife-wielding OR has a *tone* and carries a threat. It wants you to comply. Or else.

AND also has moods. A spectrum of AND's moods looks like this:

- Calm
- Pensive
- Straightforward
- Solid
- Self-Evident
- Open
- Encouraging
- Enthusiastic
- Inspired
- Awe-Struck

A quiet AND feels calm and contemplative, while a loud AND feels energizing and possibly astonishing. Regardless of mood, AND always has an underlying quality of positivity and potential.

Sometimes, people miss AND entirely because it can be so straightforward. AND isn't putting on a show. It's not cajoling or manipulating or criticizing. It's just telling you how it is—and how it could be.

AND comes with open arms. It carries invitations—not weapons. AND isn't mad if you don't take the invitation or come to the party. AND will keep generating possibilities. Those possibilities might feel tiny or colossal, but they always feel genuine.

Once you train your inner ear, the voices of OR and AND will become unmistakable—especially when you contrast their tone.

OR is trying to convince you of a lie while AND is quietly offering you the truth.

Start listening for OR and AND in your daily life. Don't strain your ears; just start paying attention to the *quality and tone* of:

- Your thoughts
- Words you speak or write
- Conversations at home or work
- Discussions within your community
- Discourse online or in the media

You'll start to pick up on the (often unconscious) background energy of speech. This is an amazing superpower when you apply it to *learning about your own life*. It's also an incredible liability if you use it to judge, analyze, or control others.

That leads me to a brief warning before we proceed.

For Your Ears Only

As you practice listening for OR and AND, your powers of perception will grow. Please use this wonderful gift to listen to *yourself*.

Don't parade around peering into other people's lives and truths. That would be arrogant and misguided. I know because I went through that phase many years ago. Once you know how to listen for truth, it's tempting to try to *use it as a skill*. As much as truth can be a magic wand, it's dangerous to pose as a fairy godmother.

Here's an example. Back in the early days of my career, a PhD student was sitting in my office asking for advice on how to navigate a difficult situation with her supervisor. She was talking about how eager she was to resolve the conflict and how excited she was to finish her dissertation research. But underneath her words, there was a neon sign exclaiming, "*I don't want to be here. I don't even want a PhD. I don't want any of this.*" Her spoken words didn't match her truth. So, her primary conflict wasn't actually with her supervisor. Her primary conflict was with herself.

At the time, I was so pleased with myself for seeing the truth that I just barreled forward and said something blunt like, "*It sounds to me like you don't actually want to be in this program or get a PhD at all.*" My sentence was technically true, but it was profoundly misguided. I felt my misstep immediately. The student's eyes welled up with tears, and I could feel a door slam shut inside her.

When we sit with another person's deep truths, it's not uncommon for tears to flow. Sometimes, they are tears of grief, and sometimes, they're tears of relief—both of which can be profoundly healing. But in that long-ago moment in my office, the student was fighting back tears of embarrassment. I had exposed a truth too quickly without the requisite trust. The student didn't want that truth exposed, so she slammed an internal door and hid it away more forcefully.

My desire to help had backfired. Not only had I strained the nascent trust between us, but now her feelings were hidden behind a steel door. I had inadvertently made it *harder* for the student to access her own truth, much less share it with others.

I tell this story not to discourage you from deep and meaningful conversations with those in your life. By all means, listen for OR and AND in many different contexts. Just be aware that you may be tempted to "use" these newfound skills to "help" others. Resist the urge!

The situation with my student taught me two critical lessons. First:

Perceptiveness can be a weapon unless it is paired with deep humility.

Truly being of service to others requires an incredible amount of discipline, devotion, and preparation.

For now, my advice is to start exploring how OR and AND work in *your life* (which the next chapters will help you do). As you begin to divest from OR and nourish AND in your own thinking and living, you will naturally begin to offer a different kind of support to those around you.

Which brings me to the second lesson:

Go in before you go out.

Helping others can spring naturally from deep compassion and caring. It can also ooze dangerously from self-protection or self-avoidance. Sometimes, we "go out" to help others because it feeds our self-image of being a Good Person. Other times, we "go out" to avoid aspects of ourselves that we don't want to see. It's often much easier to focus on the faults of others than to reflect on our own.

So, we need to retrain ourselves to "go in" first.

If we cultivate an honest practice of inquiry, we see ourselves more clearly. Then, we are more likely to shine—rather than ooze—when we engage with others.

Back in the day, when the graduate student left my cramped office, I didn't follow her with a muddled apology. Instead, I sat myself down and reflected. I didn't pretend I was in the right, nor did I wallow in guilt. I simply looked clearly at the misstep.

By first reflecting *on* myself *by* myself, I was able to later repair my relationship with the student in a much kinder and more straightforward way. I also was able to rewire the ways I listen and respond to others, which would set the stage for my coaching work many years later.

The moral of the story?

Don't rush *out* to be the hero. Stay *in* and get to know yourself. You'll be glad you did.

Choose Your Adventure

This entire chapter can be summed up in one line:

Stay humble. Stay open. Stay curious.

Looking inside can feel scary. After all, we've spent years building fortresses, moats, and labyrinths to hide our secrets, fears, and wounds.

But wonderful things can happen once we start visiting those hidden places. We release our psyches from dungeons of our own design. We recover an incredible amount of energy. We stop being afraid of ourselves. We start experiencing true freedom, understanding, and joy.

Inquiry is always a choose-your-own adventure. You get to choose the temperature of your bath, the color of your journal, and the depth of your dive. Trust yourself, and let's get to it.

PART III

Deepening *And*

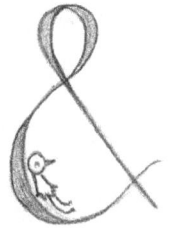

CHAPTER 7

Divesting from OR

Exposing OR

Let's get specific about where in your life OR is running the show. Because, to OR, it's definitely a show.

OR wants you—and your life—to look a certain way. It cares more about your cultivated persona than your naked truth. More about your constructed identity than your wild inspiration. More about your self-righteous pride than your whole-hearted delight.

OR is very happy with the status quo. It's actually the architect of your status quo. It's trying to keep you safe and protected, but in doing so, it's squeezing the breath out of your lungs and the joy out of your life.

The good news is that OR has a specific signature in our lives. OR thrives on conflict, constraint, criticism, control, and conformity. You can use this signature to shine a light on where OR has you tied up backstage in the theater of your life.

It may not be pretty. Resist the temptation to be hard on yourself. We've all got Or nestled away in the caverns of our inner theater. Be brave and call them into the spotlight.

Don't Hide the Madness

A few years ago, while wandering a small island in Indonesia, I came upon a round wooden sign nailed to a post on someone's porch. The island wasn't a touristy or new age-y place. So, finding this particular sign, written in English, felt like, well, a *sign*.

The sign was simple and unadorned, with just one sentence written in bright turquoise paint:

DON'T HIDE THE MADNESS.

I know I told you that four of my favorite words in the English language are "*I changed my mind.*" Well, "*Don't hide the madness*" is another four-word gem.

Every one of us is at least a bit crazy. Every one of our families is at least a little unhinged. And lord knows, our world is more than a bit deranged.

But we are taught to repress our crazy. Our persona, ego structure, and defense mechanisms have largely developed to hide the madness. We typically don't look at the most difficult aspects of our psyches, talk about the most painful secrets in our families, or grapple with the most entrenched distortions in our society.

And this doesn't serve us well.

Anything we avoid, hide, repress, or suppress has a way of running the show from backstage. We think we are side-stepping what we find painful, but we are actually augmenting its power.

There are doorways to the depths in every moment (and prompts to crack open those doors in the coming sections). Don't be shy about taking a peek. It turns out that hiding the madness also diminishes your access to real joy.

So, let's look at where OR has made itself comfortable in the shadows of your life.

The upcoming activities will give you a window into OR's tactics and help you find the places in your life most impacted by OR's negativity. OR loves cataloging things, so we'll be looking at your Catalog of Conflicts, Catalog of Constraints, and Catalog of Complaints.

I've designed these exercises so that you can do a quick first pass now and come back later (if you like) for a deeper dive. It may feel exhausting to work with OR for a full chapter, but I want you to *personally* see the cost of OR in *your* life.

Catalog of Conflicts

Focused inquiry is a powerful way to identify and disrupt long-held patterns. Let's start with a high-level overview of where OR is shaping your life.

Make a list of the main arenas of your life. Of course, there's nuance and overlap, but just take a quick first pass. You might include any or all of the following:

- Survival
- Health
- Family
- Community
- Work
- Finances
- Romance
- Sexuality
- Spirituality

Now, on a scale of 1 to 10 (with 1 being minimal and 10 being extreme), how much conflict do you feel in each arena of your life? Don't worry about whether the conflict is more internal (worries in your mind) or external (friction in your life). Just go with your instinct and write the first number that comes to mind next to the category name.

Now, write a single sentence summarizing the main conflict for each category. You might write, "Family: low-grade tension with my brother," or "Work: ready for something new but scared to quit my job," or "Health: extreme pain sapping my will to get up in the morning," or "Romance: feel lost and confused but don't know why." Keep your assessments simple.

Now that you've taken a first pass on conflict, let's look at other OR indicators. Reflect on each of the questions below.

In what areas of your life do you feel:

- the most tight and **constrained**?
- the greatest desire to **control**?
- the strongest need to **conform**?
- the most **criticized** (or tendency to criticize)?
- especially isolated or **compartmentalized**?
- particularly defined by sacrifices or **compromises**?

For each question, go back to your list and add stars next to the life arena where the feeling applies. There's no limit to how many or few stars you add. Just do it quickly and intuitively. (And feel free to add a "maybe" category using a check mark or little squiggle.)

What you have now is a quick self-assessment of OR's footprint in your life. What are your key takeaways? Are indicators of OR equally spread—or unequally distributed—across your life? Are there arenas where you are surprised to find OR lurking or lacking?

This high-level look at *where* OR lurks in your life will help you next to zoom in on *how* OR maintains its stronghold. You can go deeper into your Catalog of Conflicts if you like (for example, with stream-of-consciousness writing on any of the questions above). You can also just use it as motivation to *start paying attention* to the arenas of your life that are most disrupted by OR.

Remember, *noticing what's true* is more than half the work for personal transformation.

The best way to break habits of thought is to see them clearly.

Once you start paying attention to *where* OR is lurking, you'll start gaining potent insights into *how* OR operates in your daily life.

Now let's zoom in on some of the specific limiting beliefs OR keeps whispering in your ear.

Catalog of Constraints

OR loves to create conflict within—and between—arenas of our lives.

One of the ways OR does this is by trying to bind us into rigid roles that it claims are mutually exclusive. OR says you can only be (or have) one thing OR another but not both.

We looked at some examples earlier:

- I can be a good parent OR have a successful career.
- I can choose a noble calling OR make a lot of money.
- I can be fiercely independent OR find a loving relationship.
- I can take care of myself OR take care of others.

OR pits key arenas of your life against each other (family versus career, finances versus leisure, spirituality versus sexuality).

Why does OR do this? Because OR truly believes that you are limited.

According to OR, you never have enough capacity, opportunity, or support.

OR's fierce belief in *lack* and *scarcity* not only creates conflict in your life but also has a chilling effect on your hopes and dreams.

Let's look at how this works.

Make a quick list of ten things you want or desire, starting with:

I want to...

As always, write what comes to mind—small or large, rational or outrageous. You may have "*I want to make a million dollars*" or "*I want to hike the Camino de Santiago in Spain*" or "*I want to get a teacup poodle*" or "*I want to be free of back pain*" or "*I want to find true love.*"

It takes courage to say what you really want, so go for it.

Now, go through and add a big BUT after each item and the reason you tell yourself each desire is out of reach. Now your list will read something like:

- I want to make a million dollars, BUT I don't have any lucrative skills.
- I want to hike the Camino de Santiago in Spain, BUT I'm out of shape and can't afford it.
- I want to get a teacup poodle, BUT my life is too unstable, and my partner hates dogs.
- I want to be free of back pain, BUT I've tried everything, and nothing helps.
- I want to find true love, BUT true love doesn't even exist.

BUT is a close cousin of OR (in fact, we could rephrase all of these sentences with OR (*"I need to be rich OR I can't..."*).

How do all those BUTs make you feel? And how easy was it to generate them?

What I want you to see is how quickly OR jumps in to block your dreams. OR leads with constraint, not creativity. So, we end up feeling despondent and powerless, and it happens in an instant.

You are going to say, *"But, Bree, all those BUTs are true! I don't have lucrative skills and my partner can't stand pets and the world is a cruel place where seeds of love get squashed."*

And I will raise one eyebrow.

And then you will get mad and say, "*I AM limited and constrained. It's shallow and selfish and unrealistic to think I can get what I want. It's just not how the world works.*"

And I will raise the other eyebrow.

And then you'll get very quiet because you'll have just heard the voice of OR coming out of your own mouth. You'll realize that:

Every time you say (or think), "*I AM limited and constrained,*" you become more limited and constrained in your thinking and in your living.

I'm not saying there aren't real challenges in your life. I'm saying that sometimes you turn your struggles into shackles.

The danger of all this internalized constraint is that you start limiting your actual options in your actual life with a preemptive BUT.

Now that you've primed the pump, listen for BUT in your daily life. Notice when you think, say, or hear BUT. It's a quick way to catch OR jumping into the driver's seat.

We'll return to your Catalog of Conflicts and Catalog of Constraints in the next chapter so that you have some specific tools for transforming OR to AND.

In the meantime, let's look at one last particularly insidious form of OR.

Catalog of Complaints

In Part I of our journey, we looked at some key ways that OR rules our lives. We talked about how OR loves to set everything up as a binary battle:

· Good OR bad
· Right OR wrong
· Pleasure OR pain
· Strong OR weak
· Worthy OR unworthy

A major problem with binary OR-thinking is that it takes *a ton* of your mental, emotional, and psychic energy:

First, it puts you on the offensive because you are constantly judging everything and everyone (including yourself) as good or bad (or right or wrong or strong or weak).

Second, it puts you on the defensive because you are constantly trying to prove to everyone (including yourself) that you're good (or right or strong or worthy).

Essentially, OR-thinking makes you run offense and defense at the same time in an unwinnable game.

Think you're above all this? I challenge you. Try to make it through a day (or an hour) without judging or criticizing something or someone. You may think your judgments are accurate—or even necessary. That's irrelevant right now. I just want you to see that you have a *habit* of judging, and you are *feeding that habit* every day.

Sometimes, when I'm facilitating a workshop, I challenge participants to refrain from complaining about anything for a twenty-minute coffee break. No snide comments about the quality of the coffee. No cynical quips about having too much work or too little sleep. No disparaging remarks about bosses or spouses. No self-deprecating banter about being not good enough. Nada.

It's humbling. Folks come back dumbstruck and say things like, "*I had no idea how much of my energy I use to complain,*" or *"If I stopped complaining, I wouldn't even know what to talk about."* But they also come back grateful and excited. Once they see how they have been feeding a judgment machine, they have a newfound motivation for change.

Okay, now it's your turn. What do you love to complain about? Make a messy, honest list of the things you love to judge and criticize.

Let your catalog be entirely subjective. One person might open with *"lazy people and vegans,"* while another writes *"workaholics and meat-eaters."* Start right now, and feel free to add to the list whenever you hear your inner critic (or outer judge) rear up.

This inventory reveals something important about the role of OR in your life.

If you judge people you perceive as lazy, you may be working overtime to be *seen* as hardworking. Yes, you might actually be hardworking. But remember that OR cares as much about perception as reality. So, you now have an *identity* as a hard worker that you need to spend a lot of psychic energy protecting.

Let's take another pass at this from a different direction.

How do you most want to be seen by others? Be honest and make a list of at least three desirable attributes. For example:

- Kind
- Successful
- Attractive
- Wise

Now, next to each word, write its opposite. Don't shy away from the first words that pop to mind:

- Kind/mean
- Successful/loser
- Attractive/ugly
- Wise/ignorant

Once again, if OR has its way, you'll spend a huge amount of time and effort cultivating a *persona* around your virtues. You'll constantly be trying to prove your kindness, wisdom, and beauty and trying to hide anything you consider mean, ugly, or ignorant.

That could work out okay except for two glaring problems: First, proving and hiding are both exhausting. Second, you're fighting reality.

Because, in reality, you can never be good without bad, light without dark, or pleasant without unpleasant.

I'll demonstrate. Take one pair of opposites from either of your lists above and write them as sentences. You could start with one of these pairs:

I am hardworking.	*I am lazy.*
I am kind.	*I am a jerk.*
I am successful.	*I am a loser.*
I am spontaneous.	*I am rigid.*

OR wants to put a big loud OR between each of these pairs. OR believes that you have to be lazy OR hardworking, beautiful OR ugly, worthy OR unworthy.

Let's prove OR wrong. Write down specific evidence for BOTH sides of your pair. Start with material just from today, for example:

I am hardworking.	*I am lazy.*
I wrote for longer than planned.	*I didn't take the dogs for a walk.*
I dug holes for the new fenceposts.	*I didn't finish building the fence.*
I stayed up late cleaning the house.	*I ate cereal instead of cooking dinner.*

Reading these examples won't do much for you. The magic comes from finding your own.

You'll notice a few things as you make your list. First, you'll notice that it's pretty easy to find evidence in your life for wildly different—and even opposing—claims about your-self. Second, you'll find that it's pretty hard to find conclu-sive evidence about any category.

Is it objectively good and virtuous to stay up late cleaning? Or is it objectively bad and lazy to eat cereal for dinner? Nope, they are all subjective value judgments.

You'll probably be forced to conclude that you really have no idea if you are good or bad, hardworking or lazy, spon-taneous or rigid. Sure, you have tendencies, and you also cultivate specific attributes, but the situation is far less clear than OR would have you believe.

I'm not saying this to cut you down or take away your favor-ite affirmation. You *are* wise and beautiful and successful and kind. It's just that you are also (at least occasionally) their opposites. Once you reconcile to that reality, you will have way more energy to devote to your actual values and virtues. You'll also carry less judgment and defensiveness. And you'll be able to better intuit the best course of action in any given situation without your identity clouding your judgment.

Let's have a brief look at the consequences of trying to always maintain an identity as a good person.

The Dangers of Being a Good Person

I recently met a woman in a grocery store bathroom. She was wearing a black T-shirt emblazoned with huge white block letters that said, "BE A GOOD PERSON."

She was also up to her elbows in the sink, trying to wash dog poop off her arms. She had just tried to rescue two dogs on the side of the highway, and it had gone disastrously wrong.

It reminded me of a situation with my friend Joe some years ago.

Joe is a consummate animal lover with a house full of well-loved rescue critters. One summer, Joe noticed a feral mama cat and her four kittens living under a nearby outdoor shed. Worried that the cats wouldn't survive on their own, he asked if I would help catch the cat family and find them homes.

My intuition at the time was a loud and clear "No." My stomach hurt, and my heart tightened just thinking about the prospect. I had no idea why I felt such clarity, but it was visceral.

In the end, I overrode my intuition. After all, Joe was just trying to be a Good Person, and surely I could take a few minutes out of my day to be a Good Friend.

When I look back, it's clear that my motivation was corrupted. Not only was I going against my *inner clarity*, which has devastating consequences, but I also wasn't being honest with myself—or Joe—about our friendship. We had drifted apart that year, and instead of addressing the situation directly, I was just nursing a low-grade sense of guilt for being out of touch.

So, when I met Joe at the shed, I wasn't actually being a good friend. Instead, I was subconsciously looking to *prove* I could be a Good Friend.

When I saw the kittens under the shed, I had a physical reaction that mirrored my original intuition. Again, my heart clenched, and I felt a wave of nausea. It was like the hand of the universe grabbed my shoulders and wouldn't let me get within ten feet of the shed. I had no idea why, but I couldn't help the cat rescue effort.

A few things happened in the moments after I stepped back from the shed. First, the mama cat got scared and darted across the road. She was hit and killed by a passing car. As I found a resting place for her, Joe managed to catch the remaining kittens. Joe gave them a loving home outside of town, but all four were killed by coyotes or mountain lions that year.

I know it's a depressing story, but I found the lesson to be profound.

There's a big difference between being an authentically loving friend and *trying to appear so*. Trying to appear to be a Good Friend doesn't make you one. The same is true for any other virtue. Any time we *falsely perform* a role (Good Friend, Good Person, Good Parent, etc.), we put ourselves and others at risk.

I'm not saying that we shouldn't strive toward lofty values or cultivate high morality. I'm saying that our character development needs to come from the *inside.*

Our need to prove our worth always comes from OR-thinking. And it never leads us to a true open-hearted expression of our values and virtues.

When we stop listening to our inner truth and start donning external identities, things go wrong. Friendships fray, cats die, and we are left feeling sick with ourselves. When we listen deeply to ourselves, others, and the moment, there is guidance available at every turn.

So instead of wearing T-shirts that tell others to BE A GOOD PERSON in all capital letters, we would do well to turn inward and see where we might be trying to prove what we are (or what we are not).

The Cost of OR

At this point, the cost of OR should be clear.

The way you think and the way you live are intimately tied. If you are feeding OR thoughts, you are growing an OR life. And OR will happily spend the rest of your life cataloging your conflicts, constraints, and complaints.

OR's negativity drains your life force by making you feel:

- Angry about the past
- Unsatisfied with the present
- Hopeless about the future

Not a great combination.

The good news is that *feeling* the cost of OR gives you motivation for change. Let's use that motivation to shift OR to AND.

Before we do, I'd like to caution you not to try to fling OR away quickly like a crumpled and stained napkin. Slow down. We've got old habits that are burrowed in deeply.

Give yourself time to see OR for what it is—a sad and defensive aspect of your psyche that has been doing its best to protect you. Break up on good terms.

The best break-ups lead to great friendships. OR will continue making appearances in your life. You won't hand OR the keys to the car anymore, but you might still go out for coffee. A little understanding goes a long way.

Getting to know your habits of OR-thinking is an incredible journey of self-discovery. Once you are willing to see OR without guilt, shame, or self-judgment, extraordinary things happen.

OR may even become an unlikely ally in your journey, letting you know when fear begins to narrow your vision. After all, recognizing that you're feeling limited by OR is the first step toward AND.

And if you feel a little tired from spending a whole chapter with OR, maybe you could use a nice, hot bath. Just saying.

CHAPTER 8

Investing in AND

Welcoming AND

AND is ready for you.

Actually, AND has always been ready for you. But you also need to be ready for AND.

Once we feel the cost of OR in our lives, we start naturally craving AND. We long for freedom, openness, and possibility. The longing itself is a gift from AND. It's AND's way of saying, "*How 'bout something new?*"

Remember, AND is all about invitations. AND never judges you for where you are or where you've been. AND doesn't think you need to be a better version of yourself before starting the conversation. AND is ready right now.

So, maybe it's time to welcome AND. You don't need to plan a fancy spread or fabulous guest list. AND is very happy to have a quiet chat with you here and now. In fact,

AND doesn't really want anyone else invited to the party quite yet. AND first wants to get to know you.

Feeling Shy

AND is the central inspiration for this book. I love how AND points the way to deeper truths, higher values, and more expansive possibilities. I love AND's generosity. I love AND's invitation toward more openness, joy, and spontaneity.

Yet, even with all that love, I felt some resistance when I started writing this chapter—where I go deeper into the meaning of AND. How fascinating.

So, I did what any card-carrying AND-er would do: I sat down with the foursquare.

I grabbed a blank index card and my favorite Blackwing pencil and took a few centering breaths. Then, I considered the four questions:

1. **What's going on right now?**
2. **What am I afraid of?**
3. **What's really true?**
4. **What's my way forward?**

Lo and behold, AND gave me some practical and profound advice. Here's a quick synopsis of our conversation:

1. **What's going on right now?**

- I'm resistant to starting the AND chapter.

2. What am I afraid of?

- I won't do AND justice.
- I'm not up for the job.
- There are other things I need to do first.
- AND doesn't want to be exposed.
- It will feel weird to share AND publicly with the world.

3. What's really true?

- AND *is* actually a bit shy and doesn't want to be overexposed.
- AND doesn't like a bright spotlight or a loud interrogation.
- AND likes curiosity and intimacy.
- AND is excited to meet new people.
- AND wants me to write.

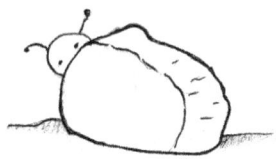

4. What's my way forward?

- Write. Now.

I want you to notice a few things about this conversation.

First, it was an *unplanned conversation*. All I knew when I started the foursquare was that I was feeling resistance. I didn't know why, and I didn't know what to do about it. I sat down with a blank card—both literally and figuratively.

I approached the inquiry with curiosity and openness, not judgment or impatience.

Second, I let the questions guide me and answered them in order. I didn't jump to any conclusions. If I had skipped the middle two questions and gone straight from "*I'm having resistance to writing*" to "*Write now,*" the process wouldn't have worked. In fact, I likely would have had *more* resistance to writing because I would have been trying to force a solution without understanding my fears or the bigger picture. The magic is the *internal* transition from OR to AND.

Third, there's a fascinating contrast between my list of fears and my list of truths. The fears are mostly self-centered: They are about *me* and what *I* want. The truths are not: They are about AND and what AND needs. I didn't plan it this way. It was a lesson that emerged in that specific moment. It's as if the process was saying, "*Hey honey, this isn't really about you. Let's get back to your deeper commitment to be of service.*" This helped my resistance dissolve and my energy return.

Finally, the way forward was extremely straightforward: "*Write. Now.*" The words were simple, but the message was meaningful. It wasn't just a command to write; it was an affirmation that the time was right.

It was also an invitation to write differently. AND had reminded me that the *feeling* of this chapter needs to be less like a brightly lit stage and more like an intimate dinner party.

Because I have deep faith in the OR-to-AND process, I always obey AND's suggested way forward. AND could have said, *"Today is not the day."* or *"Change the book title."* or *"Make pancakes first."* and I would have listened. I know that any direction coming from AND contains wisdom and possibility.

That said, AND did not tell me to make pancakes. AND said, *"Write."* So here we are.

Transforming the Catalogs

In the last chapter, we made Catalogs of Conflicts, Constraints, and Complaints. OR loves catalogs because they provide a way to keep track of grievances and reasons to stay self-righteous or resentful.

In fact, OR would be thrilled to stand center stage and read the catalogs aloud to an enormous audience—telling everyone how things should be. OR would emerge wearing a fancy hat and begin by declaring, *"Have I told you, dear sir, how much I hate goldfish? No?! What an outrage! Let me begin at the top of my soliloquy again so you truly understand how goldfish are ruining our society."*

OR would give bonbons to anyone who agreed and would secretly kill the detractors. No matter how brightly lit OR's theater, OR always maintains a dark and sinister backstage.

In contrast, Aɴᴅ isn't interested in making speeches or presenting well-documented justifications. Aɴᴅ doesn't want a list of reasons why you should stay angry. Aɴᴅ is happy for folks to come and go freely. Aɴᴅ doesn't care whether people agree because agreement isn't the most important thing. Frankly, it's a little boring when everyone has the same opinion.

Aɴᴅ cares about truth and freedom and possibility, and we won't find freedom by pretending that Oʀ doesn't exist. We need to be honest: Oʀ loves cataloging resentments and counting beans. Meanwhile, Aɴᴅ will eat all the beans for breakfast so you don't have to keep counting them for the rest of your life.

When we are open to Aɴᴅ, we begin relating to our challenges in a new way. We start looking for creativity even in the face of challenge. So, let's revisit our three catalogs with Aɴᴅ by our side.

Picturing Possibilities

To feel the freedom of AND, we need to loosen the constraints of OR.

AND doesn't want to shred OR's lists and catalogs—AND wants to *transform* them. AND teaches us to look for possibility even in the most entrenched conflicts.

Let's learn how by taking another look at our life arenas.

Get out your AND journal or grab a piece of blank paper (and maybe some colored pencils) so you're ready to write your category names from the last chapter (survival, health, family, community, work, finances, romance, sexuality, spirituality, and anything else you'd like to include).

This time, please don't make your list linear! Write the words intuitively any way and anywhere you like on the page. You might find that you write some categories big and others small, some clustered together and others alone, some higher and others lower. Go ahead; write down your life arenas now.

In just a few moments, you've created an intuitive map of your life. Now, step back and see what you learn. There's always something new to observe.

For example, in my current version, I put "family" and "community" at the very bottom of my page. They seemed to create stability as a foundation in my life. I was also surprised to see that "romance," "sexuality," and "spirituality" were all close together at the top of my page. Those arenas might not all seem related, but they share a certain quality of expansion in my life. And once I put words on paper, I saw a gap. My relationship with the desert has become so central that it wanted its own category. Adding the word "place" made my constellation more complete.

Now, go back to your page and ask which categories could use a deeper dose of ᴀND. Circle or star some. Underline or connect others. Again, just be intuitive.

Finally, ask the highlighted categories what they need from you. Listen for quiet, simple answers. Some might ask for specific types of attention or action. Others may just need time and patience. Doodle or annotate any way you like.

You have now officially transformed your Catalog of Conflicts into a Picture of Possibilities. Instead of assuming the big arenas of your life are rife with conflict and compromise, you're actually listening to what's needed. Often, we don't need to take apart and rebuild our lives. Rather, we just need to shift our attention away from limitation and toward possibility.

You can always dive deeper into the conversation by using the four questions. If you're in a contemplative mood, pick one right now and go through the Oʀ-to-ᴀND process.

1. *What's going on in this arena of my life?*

2. *What am I afraid of in this arena of my life?*

3. *What's really true in this arena of my life?*

4. *What's my way forward in this arena of my life?*

If you'd prefer to move on for now, the four questions are there for you anytime.

Choosing Creativity

Next up, let's revisit your Catalog of Constraints. For this list, you wrote down your desires and then gave OR free rein to shut them down. Now, we're going to revisit the exploration with an AND mindset. Pick one constraint from your list (or write a new one) that feels alive. You might have:

- I want to make more money BUT I feel stuck in my current job.
- I want to hike the Camino de Santiago BUT it's expensive, and I'm out of shape.
- I want to write a memoir BUT I never make time to write.
- I want to find a new relationship BUT I can't stand online dating.

Now, in each sentence, cross out the BUT and replace it with AND. The physical act of crossing out BUT and writing in AND is important. It flips a switch in your mind. Do it.

Now, add a new SO clause to each sentence that *proposes a specific action you could take that honors both prior clauses.*

Make your SO clauses almost comically specific. Feel free to brainstorm possibilities that run the gamut from trivial to edgy to downright ludicrous. Include at least one idea that is actionable *today.* Sprinkle in a little fun if you can. Here are a few examples to inspire your thinking:

I want to write a memoir AND I never make time to write SO I will invite my three closest friends—and their favorite mugs—over tonight, and we will drink tea and each write 500 words.

I want to hike the Camino de Santiago AND it's expensive AND I'm out of shape SO I will ask my relatives to gift travel funds for my birthday and do 100 lunges per day while looking at a map of Spain—starting today.

I want to make more money AND I feel stuck in my current job SO I will email three business contacts today and ask if they might have some consulting work for me, and if no one responds by 8:14 a.m. tomorrow, I'll email my current boss asking for a raise.

This AND-SO exercise encourages you to think without limits. It demonstrates that you have options—not just vague future hopes but specific, actionable possibilities. If you find possibilities you like, that's great. If not, you aren't bound to any of these outcomes. You are simply kickstarting your creativity.

Once you give yourself permission to consider creative solutions, your gears will start turning in the background. You may wake up in the middle of the night with the perfect idea to pursue.

So, remember, OR can only count to two. Once OR adds the second BUT clause, it's done. Game over. Dream broken.

AND thrives on threes. Once AND adds a third SO clause, it's just getting started. Game on. Dream bigger.

Now, you have a specific practice you can use in daily life. Anytime OR starts adding to your Catalog of Constraints, change BUT to AND, then add SO.

And if you want a bonus challenge, bring together multiple desires to make a mega-desire that is bigger and bolder than any of your originals. Perhaps you'll write, "*I want to fly first class to Spain and hike the Camino de Santiago and write a memoir about it.*"

Don't worry if OR says your big dreams are impossible. AND is ready and excited for the challenge.

Family, Farm, and Fame

I want to underscore how powerful this simple AND-to-SO approach can be. Time and again, friends, students, and clients report that this one practice has rewired their minds and changed their lives.

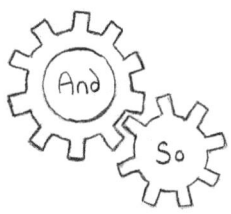

I often facilitate OR-to-AND workshops at large conferences where it's easy for participants to feel lost. The *content*

of the conference might be interesting, but the *culture* of the conference might be rife with Oʀ.

At large professional meetings, there isn't usually a dedicated place to grapple with difficult questions. That's where Aɴᴅ comes in. Regardless of the topic of the conference, I can use the Oʀ-to-Aɴᴅ process to ignite new ways of thinking. We may focus on job searches, creativity slumps, leadership development, strategic planning, or any other specific topic. But what we are really doing is learning a *general process* for shifting constraint to possibility.

At one recent conference, I had a hundred early-career professionals eating lunch together and grappling with how to better integrate their personal and professional goals. Over sandwiches and salads, they explored the hopes and dreams that seemed the most difficult to actualize.

I always use an opening activity to gauge the temperature of the room, so I already knew this particular audience had a lot of pessimism about the future and skepticism about being able to integrate their personal and professional goals.

So, it was inspiring to feel the group's unbridled enthusiasm as they began to cross out Oʀ and replace it with Aɴᴅ. A few participants shared fabulous examples with the group, and then there was a natural lull in the conversation. At that moment, I felt a kind of electricity in the very back of the room, so I asked, "*Is there anyone who hasn't spoken yet today but found a surprising Aɴᴅ?*"

There was a pause, and I thought I might have been wrong. But then, a woman at the back table stood up.

Often, in workshop settings, people are nervous to share their truth. They don't know how their words will sound out loud to their own ears, much less to a room full of colleagues. Folks might speak quietly, give a little pre-amble explaining their thoughts, or subtly diminish their own ideas. It's my job to create trust, nurture emerging ideas, and stoke participants' confidence in themselves.

So, I was surprised when the woman who stood up said in a strong, clear voice, "*I want to be a complete rock star in my career AND I want to raise a huge family on an enormous farm.*"

That sentence may not be revolutionary for you. But it was for her. She was breaking the hold of OR. She didn't want an adequate career. She wanted a rock-star career. And she didn't want a modest home life. She wanted a huge family on an enormous farm. She was no longer willing to compromise or tone herself down. She shared her dream and then sat back down to compose the final clause for her sentence.

And here's the magic. The SO clause makes your AND real. It provides direction and fuels action. Adding SO replaces a vague desire (*I want*) with a concrete plan (*I will*).

By the time you have written your SO clause, you have made another great leap. You have taken something that seemed impossible and made it far more than possible. You've planted the seeds for its fruition.

My back-row participant may have arrived at the workshop feeling like this: *My personal and professional dreams are in great conflict. I probably won't get what I want in either arena. Even if I get close to my goals in one area, it will come at a grave sacrifice in the other. I should shrink myself and my hopes down to a more manageable size, but even so, I'll probably never really be happy.*

She left saying, "*I WILL be a complete rock star in my career AND I WILL raise a huge family on an enormous farm.*"

How will she do it? How will AND help her? You'll have to stay tuned. But I'd bet the farm she does.

Observing Opposites

One more to go! It's time to recast your Catalog of Complaints.

In the last chapter, you made a list of things you judge. Maybe you can't stand people you consider lazy, hypocritical, or fake. And maybe you spend a lot of energy trying to be hardworking, consistent, and authentic.

Any time you're trying to be one thing and NOT another, you're on a collision course with reality. To be whole, you

can't keep denying half. So, here's your next radical act of AND—accept your contradictions.

Pick any three of the polarities you listed as complaints in the last chapter. Now write a big fat AND between the two sides.

- I am kind AND I'm a jerk.
- I am beautiful AND I am hideous.
- I am hardworking AND I am lazy.

Go ahead and read these out loud three times. It might feel horrifying or freeing. Either way, you've just taken a big step away from OR and moved closer to the reality of AND.

Accepting your contradictions allows a number of beautiful things to happen spontaneously.

First, you'll be less defensive.

Imagine you accidentally hurt someone's feelings. Instead of justifying your behavior and spiraling down a conversational rabbit hole, you might just say, "*Yup, I'm a jerk sometimes.*" Ironically, admitting your *capacity to be a jerk* makes you less of a jerk. Otherwise, you're a double jerk: Once when you're a jerk and again when you deny being a jerk.

Second, you'll be far less judgmental.

If you know your own capacity for laziness, rigidity, or impatience, you'll be more forgiving of those traits in yourself and in others. That doesn't mean you can't hold yourself and others to high standards. In fact, it makes it easier to be direct. Imagine saying to your team at work, "*I really value hard work AND I feel like we're missing the mark. Let's talk about what's getting in the way."* When you stop hiding your own laziness, you stop forcing other people to hide theirs. Everything gets way simpler.

Third, you'll have lots more energy to devote to your actual values and virtues.

Being honest about your fears and foibles naturally builds character and capacity. It's self-evident. Being honest with yourself and others is in itself a high virtue. Now, instead of wasting energy hiding your unsavory tendencies, you're setting a new tone. In fact, you'll find that showing your humanity is a form of leadership. When you stop pretending, your authenticity benefits all.

So, are you ready to let go of your long-held gripes and complaints? Burn them, eat them, or turn them into an ironic poem to read at your new complaint-free coffee hour.

You're now free to interface with the world as it actually is—not how you demand it should be.

Love and Paella

My daughter was an exchange student in Spain last year. After a few months, she started ending her letters: *"With love and paella, Chloe."* For the longest time, I couldn't figure out why I liked it so much. And then it dawned on me. It was a delightfully surprising AND.

In meditation and bodywork circles, it's common for folks to sign their emails with "*Love and light.*" I always find this ironic. Technically, "*Love and light*" contains the word AND. But it *implies* a big OR. It suggests that the teacher (or therapist or chef or whoever) is full of love and light and not the opposites.

The most enlightened beings I've met on planet Earth are *intimately* aware of the interplay between love and hate, light and darkness. So, "*With love and light*" always sounds a bit poser-ish to me (although not enough to want to start a Catalog of Complaints).

I'm not suggesting that we sign our emails "*With light and darkness.*" That would be absurd. Of course, we want to express—and spread—our love. I'm just saying that once we befriend AND, we don't have to pretend to be half of anything. It's time to be whole.

There's another reason I love Chloe's closing "*With love and paella.*" The two words aren't opposites at all. They illustrate that AND can bring anything at all together. That's where we're headed next.

In the meantime, I'll sign off with love and light and darkness and paella.

CHAPTER 9

Dreaming Bigger with AND

Too Much Is Just Enough

Way back in college, when my roommate Lina and I cooked a meal that came out looking weird, she used to say, "*Shapes don't taste.*" It was a sweet way to acknowledge that when things don't go as planned, we can still enjoy them. In fact, sometimes the unexpected is even more delightful.

"*Shapes don't taste*" applies to far more than messed up-looking pancakes. I find that whenever I mess things up—even if it's not dinner—I hear that refrain in my mind. It reminds me to note any missteps, ease off the judgment, and enjoy things for what they are.

As you experiment with bringing AND into your life, it may occasionally feel clunky—like the glorious meal you planned that came out looking a little strange. Enjoy the unexpected.

By transforming OR to AND, you're disrupting long-held patterns and beliefs. Switching tracks isn't always easy and may not always look pretty. Rest assured, AND doesn't mind if you try something nutty that doesn't work out. AND knows that you'll learn from your experiences, and it loves whatever shape you create.

The goal of this chapter is to encourage you to *experiment*. The exercises and prompts are designed to get you exploring new territory and possibilities in your life.

This brings us to the second gem from my college roommate, "*Too much is just enough.*" Lina used to pull this one out whenever we were teetering on the brink of going overboard.

Sure, there are times when it's literally or figuratively dangerous to go overboard. But oftentimes, we rein ourselves in prematurely. We restrict our dreams, tamp down our exuberance, and hold back from taking small risks that could offer great joy.

When I first sketched out the chapters of this book, I planned one chapter for OR practices and one chapter for AND practices—simple, parallel, and tidy. But then, AND asked for another chapter. AND wanted to offer some bonus exercises. I tried to say no, but AND held my gaze and responded, "*Too much is just enough.*"

AND would rather give too much than too little. And usually, that "too much" is actually "just enough." Because we are so accustomed to a stingy, anemic OR, the generosity of AND can seem positively outrageous, but it's not. AND knows what it's doing.

So, this bonus chapter is brought to you courtesy of AND. Let's look at how AND can help you discover outrageous possibilities in your own life. I'll give you an example from mine to kick off the festivities.

Maple Bacon

Earlier this year, I was having breakfast at a diner in Texas with my new and unlikely friend, Jake. New because we had met just months before. Unlikely because we are about as different as can be.

I'm a meditation-loving scientist from Brooklyn. Jake's a gun-loving builder from Michigan. I buy overpriced organic kombucha. Jake buys Coke. I eat corn off the cob in vertical stripes. Jake eats it in horizontal stripes, like a typewriter. You get the picture.

We were sitting in a booth at a diner named Maple Bacon, eating hash browns, when Jake said, *"You know, I've always wanted to visit all thirty U.S. baseball stadiums."*

I didn't say, *"Why?"* or *"That sounds hard."* or *"I don't like baseball."* I said, *"You know what would be fun? Let's collide our interests into a single trip."*

We started with the basics. Jake loves baseball and building things. I love teaching and writing. So, over the course of an hour, three eggs, and some orange juice, we came up with this plan:

- Let's go to all thirty baseball stadiums in a single summer.
- Let's do it by following Jake's favorite team—the Detroit Tigers—to all of their games.
- Instead of renting an apartment in Detroit, let's build a small house—by ourselves—within biking distance of the stadium.
- Instead of staying in hotels for away games, let's drive around the country in a camper.
- In every city we visit, let's offer OR-to-AND workshops and use the proceeds from the workshops to support local Little League teams.
- Let's write a book about the experience. Actually, let's write two books—one from each of our perspectives.
- Let's not show each other what we are writing until the books are published.
- Let's use proceeds from the adventure to start a scholarship fund at Bree's new nonprofit and bring even more different people, ideas, and dreams together.

We weren't creating a summer of parallel play (where Jake builds and goes to baseball while Bree writes and offers workshops). We were colliding things we both care about into a new adventure.

And it was actionable. Within a few days, we had made a website, looked at real estate, and had a great title for our books.

And then, AND said, "*Want more?*" AND had shown me an idea for an amazing summer. But then AND said, "*How about an amazing year? Or an amazing decade? How about an amazing life?*"

For AND, it's not about whether a specific plan gets executed. It's about sparking creativity. Once AND has your attention, things can go in unexpected directions. That doesn't mean you're constantly jumping from one crazy idea to another. It also doesn't mean you can't be committed to people, places, or plans. It just means that you *keep listening.*

For example, you can take everything in this story (me, Jake, corn, hash browns, baseball, building, traveling, writing, teaching, philanthropy) and arrange us into many different possible futures.

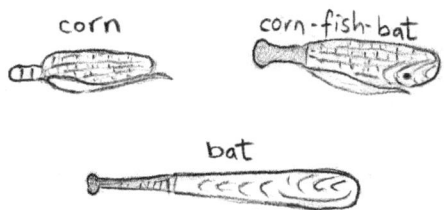

And there are other things that matter deeply to me that aren't on that list. So, the Maple Bacon session was only the beginning.

The point is that AND needed to bump me into a *mood of possibility* so that I would be interested in a bigger conversation. My job was just to say, *"Yes."*

Let's talk about ways you can foster your own mood of possibility and expand the conversation and the joy in your life.

Unexpected Connections

One theme you'll notice in this book is that AND does more than bring together opposites. AND can bring together *anything*. This is why Chloe's *"love and paella"* signoff is delightful. This is why it's fabulous to collide baseball, building, writing, and workshops. And this is why we want to shift perceived constraints into actionable possibilities.

When we shift OR to AND, we replace opposition with opportunity.

Well, it turns out we don't need to start with OR at all. We simply can bring disparate *positive* ideas together with AND.

Let's practice with a quick exercise I call Love Collisions. Instead of starting with topics that feel in tension, let's start by colliding things you care about.

Make a list of at least ten things you love. Big or small. No hierarchy. No order. Don't worry if you write five entirely trivial items before you even remember you have kids. Don't worry if you write strange, sexy, or scary things. Go with it, and don't censor!

Here are mine from a recent round of Love Collisions:

- Clay pots
- Desert lizards
- Flannel shirts
- Astronomy
- Creamed corn
- Grapefruit juice
- My kids
- Quiet churches
- Winding roads in other countries
- Being naked in the sun

Now, write each on a slip of paper. Put them in a hat (or a bowl). Pick two out randomly and lay them next to each other. Every once in a while, you'll pick two that are just really uncomfortable to put together (*being naked in the sun + my kids = yikes!*). If this happens, just toss them back and pick a different pair.

Once you have your pair laid out, write a big OR between them just to remind yourself how dead that makes you feel. Grapefruit juice OR creamed corn. Boring.

Now, put an AND between them and remember how enlivening that is. Even if they are the two most banal things in the world, AND gets our gears turning. Grapefruit juice

AND creamed corn. Mmmm... makes me want to invent a new recipe or build a strange lunch menu.

Okay, turn back to the two slips of paper you actually chose. Come up with at least three ways you could connect those two loves in your life. Don't worry if they are good ideas. Don't worry if they are feasible. Your goal is to start generating possibilities and retrain your mind to see possibilities in unexpected connections.

I like to challenge myself to come up with one small, one medium, and one large idea. Here's an example with desert lizards + flannel shirts:

- *Small: Draw a lizard wearing a flannel shirt, print it as a sticker, and give stickers to my biology students.*
- *Medium: Buy a new flannel shirt, book a trip to Baja, and wear the flannel shirt every day until I've seen three new species of lizards.*
- *Large: Start a flannel-shirt-making company and use all the profits to create scholarships for students who want to do desert lizard research.*

Am I actually going to do any of those things? Probably not. Does it make me feel a sense of possibility and potential? Absolutely. Does the exercise help spark ideas that are actually important in my life? Almost always.

How does the collision of random things spark true insight? It's simple: *YOU are the one creating the connections, so you naturally create connections that have meaning for you.*

For example, if you look past the lizards and flannel shirts, you can see where my mind went in this exercise.

· *Small: Give more to my students.*
· *Medium: Have a travel adventure.*
· *Large: Develop a scholarship program for my nonprofit.*

In less than five minutes, I went from two random things I like (lizards and flannels) to three important priorities in my life (which were not front-and-center before this exercise).

Now, we get to go deeper using our favorite method—inquiry. You can use the four questions to see if anything specific is holding you back. Or you can simply ask how to *take action* based on what you learned from your Love Collision. For example:

· *Small: How do I want to give more to my students? It's time to announce a new fall writing retreat.*
· *Medium: What feels exciting for a travel adventure? Plan a winter visit to an old friend in Greece.*
· *Large: What's the next step for my scholarship program? Host a spring donor event on my land in New Mexico.*

I love the simple whimsy—and concrete outcome—of this exploration.

Use the Love Collisions exercise anytime you feel stuck. Your love list is likely to change day to day, and so will the connections you create.

In my coaching and consulting work, I use many variations on this exercise to help people incorporate AND into their lives. For example, I might look for creative ways someone's disparate interests fit together to spark a more authentic and inspiring career direction. Or I might explore ways of bringing multiple priorities together for a strategic plan at a place of work or worship. The possibilities are endless.

Now that you're warmed up with a little creative thinking, let's revisit some specific situations in your life that could use an AND infusion.

The Third Thing

Decision-making is difficult and especially prone to OR-thinking. When we are stressed about an upcoming choice, we often take a double dose of binary thinking. First, we think we need to choose between A and B. Second, we think there is one right and one wrong path.

We don't know which option is "right," and we are terrified that we'll choose the "wrong" one, so we get paralyzed. We procrastinate and overanalyze. It's not pretty.

Let's explore a simple way to disrupt binary thinking about decision-making.

Think of a situation in your life where you feel torn between two different options. Let's call them A and B. Write these down with an OR between them.

For example:

- I can be a scientist OR an artist.
- I can move to Phoenix OR Panama.
- I can leave OR stay in this relationship.
- I can work for a company OR work for myself.
- I can paint the living room beige OR green.

OR is predictable. OR always presents two options. You can do *this* OR *that*, A OR B.

You can stay in the grip of OR for days, weeks, months, or even years. You can stress about an impending choice, make a list of the pros and cons, work yourself into a frenzy, and still stay stuck in a situation you don't like.

The problem isn't OR. The problem is believing that OR is your only option.

One simple way to disrupt this type of binary thinking is to replace OR with AND. Now we have a third option: You can do A AND B.

For example:

- I can be a scientist AND an artist.
- I can move to Phoenix AND Panama.
- I can leave AND stay in this relationship.
- I can work for a company AND work for myself.
- I can paint the living room beige AND green.

This may initially scramble your brain. How can you simultaneously leave and stay in a relationship? Or move to two different places? Don't dismiss the possibility.

Perhaps you're longing for more space from your partner but not a complete break. Perhaps you want to rotate among multiple countries. Perhaps you would absolutely love a multicolored living room.

For your particular situation, consider whether there's a creative and unexpected way to do both A and B.

Whenever we feel torn between two options, it's because, at some level, BOTH matter. If we simply choose one Or the other, we lose the chance to craft a truly unique life.

That doesn't mean you need to do A And B exactly as written. Here's where the fun begins.

Ask yourself: *What deeper desires do these two choices represent?*

You might not merge A and B exactly as you wrote them. But perhaps you need to better honor seemingly conflicting desires. Maybe you need *both* connection and solitude, *both* stability and adventure, *both* rationality and poetry.

You've been trying to choose between parts of yourself, and you no longer need to do that.

Who says you can't be a poetic farmer, a vegan gun instructor, an artsy scientist, or a Zen sex therapist? In fact, who says you even need to label or justify your choices at all?

When you make life choices, do it in a way that honors all of your dimensions.

Maybe you want a room of your own in the house you've shared with a partner for twenty years. Maybe you want to go down to 80 percent time at your current job so you can start your own graphic design business. Maybe you want to build an adobe home in the heart of Tokyo.

I don't know what you want. All I know is that it's possible.

AND creates possibility because it presents a third option.

- You can do A.
- You can do B.
- You can do *both.*

Once you add a third option, you break free of binary thinking. Now, you can consider all sorts of alternatives.

- You can do neither.
- You can do C.
- You can do 82 percent A, 17 percent B, and 1 percent C.
- You can wait to see if Q or Z is possible.

What possibilities haven't you considered in your current situation? Open up your dreaming space and let yourself be whimsical. Come up with a few new, wild, and creative options.

You don't want to live a scripted life built on binary choices. You want a life that's unique, rewarding, and *yours*.

The Watermelon Dog

Thinking outside the box—or getting out of binary thinking—is a *practice*. It requires your active engagement. And yet, once you begin looking for creative possibilities, they begin finding you. All you need to do is trust the process.

A few years ago, I was at a conference in Italy, having lunch with my dear friend Luke. The winter Tuscan sky was gorgeous, and the array of meats and melons was exquisite, but I was cranky.

I was going through a rough patch in my life, and I was explaining how lost and hopeless I felt. After years of learning how to live joyfully with AND, I felt stuck again in OR. I was facing challenging choices, both personally and professionally, and I was frustrated.

I was frustrated with myself for not finding a way forward. I was also frustrated with life. After all, I was good friends with AND now. So, why was life serving up fabulous salami and cantaloupe but no direction for my life? You can feel the grip of OR here. It's self-centered, judgmental, and blame-y.

I was laying out a *this* OR *that* diatribe when Luke interrupted me with a non sequitur, declaring, *"What you need is a watermelon dog."*

Perplexed, I said, *"Sorry, what?"*

He responded, *"You need a watermelon dog. You know, a creative solution. Something you can't plan ahead of time, but you'll know it when you find it."*

Luke knows that bringing unexpected things together jostles me out of binary thinking. And he's fabulous at random associations.

Except this association wasn't random for Luke. It turns out that through a series of strange synchronicities, he had gotten an actual dog at an actual watermelon farm earlier that year.

The phrase *"watermelon dog"* immediately became a kind of touchstone for me. It was a reminder that unexpected things happen when we have faith in the journey. I needed to trust the process, stay open to creative possibilities, and say *"yes"* when they appeared.

The strangest thing is that actual *watermelon dogs* started appearing in my life. People sent me memes of dogs sitting in watermelons. And one day, my son came home with a stuffed dog wearing a watermelon costume.

AND has a sense of humor.

It was like life was saying, *"Hey, honey, I'm working on your watermelon dog. Can you have a little patience and faith?"*

Just because we develop a relationship with AND doesn't mean that a perfect life will be served on a silver platter. A perfect life doesn't exist. An adventure does.

We need to stay open, have some faith, and let our watermelon dogs find us.

Stay in the Conversation

The moral of the watermelon dog story? *Stay in the conversation.*

AND works in mysterious ways. It's not a one-and-done method. Even when we think we know AND, we need to keep listening. Even when we are frustrated, we need to stay in the conversation. Even when we feel lost, we need to be open to finding our watermelon dog.

When you engage with AND through the exercises in the last few chapters, you're creating possibilities. What that looks like will vary. You might have immediate insights that change your direction entirely. Or you might start a deeper conversation that percolates and slowly reshapes your life.

The important thing is to have faith and don't rush yourself—or life.

There are so many ways to stay in the conversation with AND.

I encourage you to revisit the exercises in this book at any time. Even if the prompts are the same, your answers will be different, and you'll discover fresh meaning and possibility.

Even if you're not having an overt conflict, make time to explore areas of your life that could use new and creative ways of thinking.

And even when you aren't engaged in a structured AND activity, *keep listening*. AND is percolating in your life.

Over time, the AND practice and perspective will become more and more your own. You have a unique way of seeing, experiencing, and understanding life. Personalize your AND practice, and *make it your own*.

As you know, I have a penchant for four-word sentences. So, let's add these to our list of faves:

· I changed my mind.
· Don't hide the madness.
· Stay in the conversation.
· Make it your own.

However you choose to keep the conversation going is perfect. You may have times when you work with OR-to-AND intensively. And you may have times when the process is in the background as a quiet reminder. Either way, AND will be working its magic in your life and inviting you to dream bigger.

&

PART IV

Expanding AND

CHAPTER 10

The Easy Way

Expand the AND

The reality of transformation is that it's sometimes shockingly easy, sometimes painfully difficult, and always wonderfully surprising.

Regardless, it's essential to have a *relationship* with your OR-to-AND process. The maturing of any relationship always involves releasing lingering fantasies and embracing the sweetness of reality. You're now ready for a mature relationship with your own transformation.

When you first met OR, you might have thought OR was a bad guy you could avoid, vanquish, or conquer. Now, you probably realize that OR has depth. Even if OR confines, challenges, and criticizes you, OR also offers you an incredible opportunity for transformation.

Every time you encounter OR, you arrive at a doorway in your mind. That door leads to self-knowledge and self-actualization. It also leads directly to AND. When you address the pain of OR, you become open to AND.

When you first met AND, you might have thought AND was a lightweight or a happy-go-lucky fling. Now, you see that AND also has depth. AND doesn't always bring sunshine and roses but always offers expansion and possibility. AND cares about your freedom and is a partner in your transformation.

This brings us to a curious reality that both OR and AND are part of your transformation. When AND comes to dance at your party, she doesn't demand that you kick out OR. AND is perfectly happy with the reality of transformation.

So, it's time to expand the AND yet again and explore how to live maturely in an OR-to-AND journey. AND is a wonderful companion, whether times are easy or hard. Nothing needs to be left out.

This chapter is an invitation to relax, soften your gaze, and enjoy taking the easy way now and then.

Staying Loose

I love frameworks, processes, and practices. Obviously. I've just spent thousands of words sharing four squares and four questions and lots of additional practices.

Having a rigorous method is important. It provides a concrete way to engage with your own circumstance and your thoughts. I've seen the OR-to-AND approach work again and again in the lives of my students and clients—and in my own life.

And yet... there comes a time when we need to loosen up. A point when we have to let AND *work through us* rather than *work for us*.

AND doesn't like being put in a box. AND isn't going to trudge to the office every day and sit in a cubicle. AND needs to be let loose in your life.

You can still engage deeply with the four questions and the OR-to-AND practices. But you can also relax and trust that AND will work its magic in your life.

I'm sure you've felt the difference between intense and soft focus. Intense focus is absolutely necessary when we are learning something new, attempting something perilous, or attending to an emergency. But even heart surgeons, fighter pilots, and elite athletes say that true mastery also involves the ability to enter soft focus.

Soft focus allows our instincts to take over. We tap into the peripheral vision of our minds and see the big picture. Our hard-earned skills and our deeply felt intuition exist simultaneously.

The same is true with transformational practices. Focused practice is important, yet the ability to *relax* is equally essential.

Relaxation is a form of trust. When we relax with AND, we begin to develop a more natural rapport and trust.

Imagine a new romance. Usually, there's an immersive phase where you run around *doing things*. You go to the museum, have long conversations, and visit the archives of your past. Eventually, if you're fortunate, the trust and understanding deepen enough for you to relax. You can still dive deep together, but you can also enjoy a quiet meal.

Getting to know AND is like that. The real gold is when you move seamlessly back and forth between intentional practice and quiet listening.

Let's look at some ways to soften the focus.

Holding Precious Things

Did you ever catch bugs or worms or frogs when you were young? Do you remember the feeling of finding something wonderful and mysterious and wanting to take a closer look?

If so, bring yourself back to a memory where you held a small creature in your hands. If you don't have a specific memory, just imagine being a kid on a warm summer evening and catching a firefly.

Look down at your hands. What are your hands doing?

Chances are that you've cupped your hands to keep your prize from escaping. You're looking at the creature through a little hole you've made between your thumb and index finger.

You've found something exquisite and curious and new. To examine it, you need to confine it. Otherwise, the bug will fly, the lizard will skitter, or the frog will hop away.

It's like this with AND. When you start getting a taste of AND, you will want to keep it. You'll want to cup it—or squeeze it—in your hands to make sure it doesn't fly away.

But this isn't how it works. AND is like any other living thing. It has a life of its own, and it's not yours to keep. You can talk, play, and dance with it, but you can't keep it in a box. You already know that AND doesn't like boxes.

AND needs to be free to come and go. Don't try to put it in a cage and evaluate it from a safe distance. Don't use it once and then store it in a cardboard box, forgotten in the back of your closet.

As a biologist, here's my advice:

Working with AND is like holding a snake. Don't let that freak you out. Snakes get a bad rap, but they are utterly astounding creatures. Picture a friendly, nonvenomous snake that's small enough for you to handle but big enough to feel a little edgy—maybe a nice striped kingsnake that's a few feet long. If you can't picture that, flip back to my author photo—I'm holding one there.

When you hold your kingsnake, you don't make a cage out of your hands. You don't squeeze it, pin it down, or restrict it in any way. You keep both your hands relaxed and engaged. You let the snake slither from hand to hand, gently supporting its body. You can guide or follow the snake, but there is a reciprocal relationship. You are learning about the snake, and the snake is learning about you, tongue flicking.

You need to hold AND like that—gently and with respect. Allow AND to learn you.

AND is not something you get to find and keep in a cage. And that's good. We're all tired of cages. AND is also not like a firefly. It's not going to fly away as soon as you loosen your grip. That's nice, too.

You can trust AND. You can also trust yourself. You'll both be there for each other.

So, relax your hands, soften your eyes, and ease your breath. Let's look at a few examples of AND working its free-range magic.

The Unplanned AND

One recent morning, I was feeling exhausted as I sat down to write. I was sitting on my favorite red chair, gazing out the window onto a horizon of sagebrush. It was a beautiful sunny day with a gentle breeze barely stirring the leaves.

In contrast, my body was heavy, my mind foggy, and my spirit sagging. I felt an old habit of judgment and impatience rear up. I thought:

Why am I so drained again? What's wrong with me?

There isn't an actual OR in either of those sentences, but you can feel the OR energy: It's judgmental and demanding. It was essentially saying, "*You need to make progress in a certain way on a certain timeline OR you are a piece of crap.*"

The self-judgment was seductive, and for a moment, the heavy, foggy, sagging feeling intensified.

But almost instantly, as OR stormed onto the stage, AND was waiting in the wings to meet it. It was a delightful surprise because I wasn't consciously flexing the AND muscle. It just happened. My gaze was drawn just outside the window to where my little tomato and lavender plants were being rustled by the wind. I thought:

The desert is so inhospitable *AND* those plants look so strong and happy.

That tiny AND (which had nothing at all to do with me or my writing or my exhaustion) reminded me that seemingly contradictory truths coexist all the time. Without any premeditation, I then heard myself think:

I am exhausted AND I am exactly where I need to be.

And then, *I don't feel like writing AND it's time to write.*

On its own, my mind decided to break the spell of OR.

Notice all of the things I did not do in this little, everyday moment. I did not argue with the OR. I did not say, *"No, Bree, you're not a piece of crap."* I did not spend an hour deconstructing or psychoanalyzing my thoughts. I did not formally go through the four questions. I simply looked outside where AND was already waiting for me. Case closed. Spell broken. Back to writing.

Three lessons from this small moment.

First, once AND is your friend, it'll be there for you. Once you reprogram your mind to find the AND, it will start finding you.

Second, the transformation of OR to AND can become remarkably quick and simple. Sure, there will be times when you want to take a deeper dive and engage with the OR-to-AND process more intentionally to understand yourself and your situation. But oftentimes AND will just be there waiting to pop the bubble of OR.

Third, AND is not linear. AND has access to all sorts of creative doors. It might enter stage left or fly down from the rafters. The sequence of thoughts I just shared with you is amazingly personalized for how I am wired:

I am a piece of crap.

· There are tomatoes growing in the desert.
· I am ready to write.

AND knows me. It knows that the way into my heart is often through nature. In a mundane moment of self-doubt, AND created an unexpected bridge by *showing me* a concrete example of resilience. Now, when I feel despondent about picking up the pen, I'll say:

"Tomatoes can grow in the desert *AND* I can write when I'm tired."

AND might not interrupt *your* inner critic with thoughts of desert tomatoes, but I guarantee it will build unexpected bridges from OR to AND in your thinking and in your life.

So, build some trust with your new friend, and don't grip the wheel so tightly. Now that you have some experience working with AND, soften the effort and let it work naturally.

The Mundane and the Mystery

AND can move great mountains in your life, but it's also quite happy to work with you in small, everyday ways. Here's another example.

Earlier this year, I was driving home with my son Bodhi after baseball tryouts.

Bodhi's been growing up on a dirt road in a small town of 900 people in the mountains of Colorado. For a rural community, we have a phenomenal baseball program. Through many other ups and downs, Bodhi's team has been a constant in his life—until this year.

This year, Bodhi's usual team disbanded, and he was left with two options. He could play a short season with the younger kids in our small town. OR he could go out for an incredibly intense travel team in the "big city" an hour down the road.

One option was small and safe and required very little effort or commitment. The other option felt big and overwhelming. And it wasn't just about baseball. As a family, we were still figuring out how to navigate our unconventional living and parenting situation. So, Bodhi's choice was also getting tangled up in bigger questions. We were all grappling with the tension between the worn-out comfort of the status quo and the scary prospect of trying something new.

As Bodhi and I were driving home after tryouts for the travel team—with our usual eighties soundtrack in the background—we were looping through the pros and cons of his options again. In a conversational lull, I asked the basic question:

"What do you actually want?"

Bodhi responded, *"Well, I have to join the team OR not join the team."*

And I said, *"What if you didn't have to pick any of the existing options? Then what would you want?"*

Bodhi responded, *"I want to join the team AND I don't want to join the team. I wish I could 'kind of' join the team."*

Moments after the words escaped his lips, my phone rang. It was the coach from the competitive travel team with an unusual proposal.

"We don't usually do this, but we were curious if Bodhi would be interested in training with us this year but waiting until next year before joining us on the road?"

The answer was a clear and simple *"Yes."*

The point of this story is not about baseball. It's about AND's close friend—*mystery.*

I can't tell you the number of times this has happened in my own life and the lives of my students and clients.

A new and amazing *real-world possibility* appears just moments after a stubborn OR gives rise to a creative AND *internally*.

Sometimes, it's an unexpected resolution to a small question, like which baseball team to join. Sometimes, it's a life-changing solution to a colossal conflict that has plagued you for years.

These moments show the direct connection between AND-thinking and AND-living.

Let's be clear. This is not a guarantee that you will always get what you want. Nor is this an argument for a new age-y type of "manifestation" where you can make anything you want just appear with your thoughts. It's simply an observation.

When OR gives way to AND *internally*, new possibilities emerge *externally*.

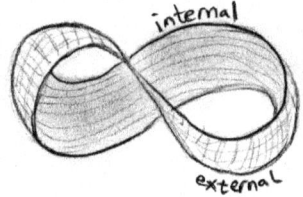

When you shift into AND-thinking, you step into a new landscape of possibilities. You see new opportunities, pursue unexpected connections, and choose novel directions.

Round House Reprise

I'll give you one more example of AND's love of synchronicity.

Earlier this year, I started a nonprofit. I was on sabbatical from the university and immersing myself deeply in the desert when a vision emerged for a retreat center in New Mexico. We'll return to the retreat center in a moment, but first, I need to catch you up on how I got to that moment.

Let's go back to when I was sick in Berkeley and felt compelled to type "round house, New Mexico" into the search bar. You may remember that an incredible home in Taos, New Mexico, popped up AND that I quickly dismissed the idea of pursuing it.

I was still addressing powerful vestiges of OR in my mind, and I simply couldn't fathom having a job in California, a family in Colorado, and a home in New Mexico. I also couldn't imagine a way to afford a new house or allow myself to consider a home of my own.

But AND's whispers kept getting louder. By the time I recovered from being sick in Berkeley, I was in my misty blue car driving to Taos.

For my entire life, I've always taken the quickest route between two points. I like to drive fast, work efficiently, and tie up loose ends before they can fray. But on that drive, I followed my intuition, took strange side roads, and backtracked whenever I felt like it. It was magnificent.

Eventually, I arrived at the round house, nestled on Blueberry Hill above Taos. I crossed the small brick courtyard, opened the carved wooden door, and stepped into the living room. As I looked out the small round window framing one perfect peak of the Sangre de Cristo Mountains, I felt like I would do *anything* to live in that house.

Which is when my friend Page, the realtor, told me that the house had gone under contract five minutes prior with another buyer.

A dam of longing and regret burst inside me. I felt like a total failure. AND had given me clear instructions, but I hadn't followed them fast enough. I blew it. I'd lost my chance.

And yet... AND has a curious way of playing the long game. AND isn't afraid of a few twists and turns and isn't always about immediate gratification.

It turns out I needed some time.

There were still some tender places where OR had its claws in my heart and wasn't letting go. I needed to address some deep-seated fears and desires before I could make a more courageous commitment to AND.

A few months later, one Tuesday afternoon at 2:35 p.m., Page sent me an email that was titled *"New on the Mesa."* When I opened the link to a property above the Rio Grande, there was no question and no hesitation.

The house was round, to be sure, but it was more than that. It was almost a spiral, like a shell. The adobe walls were supported by enormous wooden pillars carved like DNA helices. Instead of a small round window framing one peak, it had glorious floor-to-ceiling windows framing the entire mountain range. And instead of a small brick patio, the house opened onto forty acres of desert immediately adjacent to the Rio Grande.

And because the property was out of town and off the grid, I would be able to afford it on my own.

Twenty-four hours later, I was under contract. By winter, I was moving in.

For a long time, the round house was my place of retreat and reflection, silence and solitude. My kids visited occasionally; otherwise, I was gloriously alone when I spent time in Taos.

And then, one day last winter, AND said, "*AND?*"

That evening, I had a vision for a new retreat center founded on the principles of AND. The center itself would be perched in this landscape of incredible contrasts, where river meets desert meets sky. I would invite scientists, philosophers, artists, and builders to teach eclectic workshops colliding disparate themes. We would host short courses to foster the unexpected joy of getting out of your comfort zone and longer immersions to help people reimagine their lives in these epic times.

Within a few days of this inspiration, I had designed the inaugural year of programs, made a website, and started the IRS 501(c)(3) paperwork.

As I prepared to submit my paperwork, a wave of familiar doubt surfaced.

OR chimed in with the usual, *"What am I thinking?!?"*

AND responded good-naturedly, *"Not this time, my friend."*

OR persisted, arguing, *"Seriously! I don't have enough land, money, connections, or capacity to build a retreat center!"*

And that's when AND turned to face OR, made direct eye contact, and said with merriment, *"My dear friend, we simply don't have time for your negativity. Watch and learn."*

The next day, Page called to let me know that the forty-acre lot adjacent to my property was coming up for sale.

The next week, I met my new neighbor Jake (of Maple Bacon fame), who wanted to design and build the first workshop space.

The next month, I got a new business phone number and a new business P.O. box, and they were the same number. I mean, *actually* the same number.

I could go on. It all goes back to a moment when I heard *"round house, New Mexico"* in my mind. By listening and trusting AND, possibilities and synchronicities continued to emerge.

Whenever I look dumbfounded with gratitude and say, *"What are the chances?"* AND winks and responds, *"Well, honey, if you stick with me, the chances are pretty good!"*

The Living Map

Following AND through life is like following a living map that continues to evolve and update as you grow and change.

In this way, AND is way better than a simple compass. It doesn't just tell you which way is north. It helps create the landscape.

We have to take responsibility for shifting our thinking from OR to AND, but once we do that, the creativity of our lives seems to respond. Our job is to develop a meaningful and lasting relationship with AND's map of possibilities. Then, AND helps us navigate the new, uncharted territory.

Traversing the landscape of our lives with AND can be lighthearted and joyful. Sometimes, seeds just grow without a lot of fuss. Sometimes, AND rolls out a red carpet of synchronicities without us knowing why. Sometimes, things come together in wonderful and unexpected ways.

When we are relaxed and responsive, it's easier for AND to guide us. We're able to climb mountains and cross rivers. In fact, we may just find the perfect walking stick or boat waiting for us.

And yet, even when you have a vibrant relationship with AND, you will still have times when you cannot see the big picture or even the next step. As you traverse the landscape of your life, you will still have highs and lows, setbacks and successes.

After all, AND includes everything. AND isn't looking to lock you into a life of sunshine and synchronicities. AND plays a long and curvy game. AND knows that sometimes you'll pass through dark canyons and lonely nights.

So, before we wrap up, let's take a look at how to work with AND when you can't find an easy way forward.

CHAPTER 11

The Hard Way

Easy Way, Hard Way

When my kids were little, they didn't like brushing their teeth. They were too young to brush well themselves, and the dentist said we needed to do it for them. Parents brushing kid's teeth always seemed odd to me. Nobody brushed my teeth for me when I was little, and I turned out fine. Okay, let's be honest. I turned out a bit strange, but I don't think it had anything to do with a lack of toothbrushing support.

Anyway, given my ambivalence about assisting with toothbrushing, I devised a game called the Toothbrushing Show to get my kids to do a good job themselves. Picture Boris (my Fancy Restaurant alter ego) as a game show host with toddler contestants racing to brush their own teeth. Like I said, I turned out a bit strange.

As you might imagine, the Toothbrushing Show did not work well. So, once a week, their dad would brush their teeth. I always knew the ritual had started when I heard his voice from the bathroom asking:

"*Do you want to do it the easy way or the hard way?*"

The "easy way" was for the kids to relax and have their teeth brushed. The "hard way" was for them to resist as much as humanly possible. Even when approached with a playful spirit, I do not recommend brushing teeth the "hard way." But what surprised me on those evenings was that, periodically, I would hear gleeful screams wafting down the hallway:

"*Hard way! Hard way! We want the hard way!*"

I found this mystifying and wondered why on Earth anyone would want to do things the hard way if they had a choice.

Turns out, kids sometimes love the anticipation and drama of the hard way.

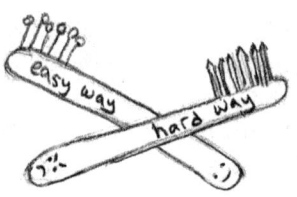

It turns out that, as adults, we also often choose the hard way.

Let's set aside toothbrushing and talk about transformation.

With our own transformation, we sometimes find an easy way, where we simply step out of boxes that have become too confining, or we pirouette gracefully out of roles that are already paper-thin.

But often, transformation is challenging. We may need to cry, scream, and pray our way out of the shackles that have rubbed our wrists raw for ages. Or we might work our fingers to the bone and find ourselves still stuck in the same situation.

Sometimes, there simply is no easy way. Other times, there is an easy way, but we can't seem to find it. And occasionally, we're simply compelled to make things as hard on ourselves as possible.

Just because things are challenging doesn't mean we're doing something wrong.

Transformation isn't always easy, but it's always *important*. Just ask carbon, as it's put under impossible pressure to form a diamond. Or ask an acorn, as it's trying to grow up and down simultaneously to become a *flipping tree*.

Don't be hard on yourself for sometimes taking the hard way.

Dry Spells and Despair

We've talked about how AND is here to stay. AND isn't skittering away like a scared lizard or flying away like a moody bug.

Yet, even when you are an AND-master, you will have times when it *seems* like AND has flown away. You will have dry spells when things feel stale and blank. You will also have stormy periods when things feel edgy and unstable. You'll need to expand AND to include these times.

If AND is working its magic in your life, you will, by definition, be charting new territory. You will be pushing your comfort zone. You will be in a new ebb and flow.

Our culture talks about "flow" like it's the best thing ever. But flow can be scary. Flow isn't something you can control. Sometimes, you'll feel like a stream rushing toward a beautiful dream—energized and powerful. At other times, you'll feel like a river breaching its banks and wreaking havoc on the surrounding flood plains—wild and terrifying. You'll need to learn to trust the unbridled energy of flow.

You'll also need to trust the wisdom of the "ebb." Our culture talks about withdrawn times like they're something to avoid at all costs. But it's foolhardy to rush or dismiss these periods. There will be dark nights, quiet days, and painful pauses. These are important interludes offering deep rest and opportunities to reset.

Once we are members of the 100 Percent Club, we must accept both the ebb and flow of our lives. We can't just harness progress and avoid pauses. In fact, just because something *appears* stalled or stagnant doesn't mean it is.

Think about the orbit of the planets. Have you heard of Mercury retrograde? It's not a new-age excuse for your computer to stop working. It's a large-scale optical illusion. Our position on Earth makes it look like Mercury slows down, stops, and turns backward in its orbit. Is Mercury really moving backward? *No.* Does it appear that way? *Absolutely.*

We sometimes fall for a similar illusion in our lives. At times, it may *look* like we have slowed down or are going backward. We judge ourselves for it and think we should never be spent, stuck, or stymied. But ebb and flow work together. You need both.

In difficult times, might you feel like AND has faded? *Yup.* Has AND actually abandoned you? *Absolutely not.*

AND is actually hard at work. Your life is and will remain a beautiful collision of opposites. You need periods of wild and periods of tame. Times of acceleration and times of retrograde. Moments of full steam ahead and moments to change tracks.

The most important thing is that you *stay interested.* If you look back at my original instructions for how to engage in Authentic Inquiry, number eight was *"Learn from everything."* The true danger of dry spells is thinking something is wrong with us and losing interest in our lives.

Once we've lost interest, we are at great risk of falling into despair.

There are times when despair finds us. Grief, suffering, and hardship are part of our lives. We all experience illness, aging, and death—our own and in the lives of those we love. The universality of loss does not make it any easier.

I've been with students and clients through many of the darkest days of their lives. The death of a parent or the tragic loss of a child. The shock of a major health diagnosis or the challenge of choosing a treatment option. The battle with depression or the lure of suicide.

AND will not protect us from pain or loss.

But I've seen again and again that AND can go to the depths. AND doesn't offer pat answers or sunshiny affirmations. AND offers truth. Sometimes, we feel that we are dying inside AND we still choose to stay alive. Sometimes, all hope feels lost AND we still enjoy a beautiful sunset. Sometimes, we feel utterly alone AND support magically arrives at our lowest moment.

Even during the darkest of times, AND offers us a way of *staying in our lives*. **It also offers a process for** *being with* **hardship and loss and** *allowing* **ourselves to be continuously transformed by our lives.**

If you'd like to work with some of the more painful aspects of your life, here are some additional prompts you can explore using the OR-to-AND process. These topics don't have a grammatical OR embedded in them, but they will guide you to material that's worthy of exploration.

Please engage with these prompts gently and with respect. The idea isn't to force yourself into uncomfortable places. The idea is to offer support to the most unsure or wounded aspects of yourself.

- A memory that still hurts or haunts
- A time when your heart was broken
- A situation where you felt betrayed
- A memory that causes you great shame
- A habit or addition that has caused you great pain
- A time when you felt shut down or dismissed
- A secret you've never told anyone
- A quiet hope that seems too good to be true
- A question for your past self
- A question for your future self
- A question for the universe

You can engage with these prompts using the four questions:

1. *What's going on?*
2. *What's my underlying fear?*
3. *What's actually true?*
4. *What now?*

Sometimes, getting beyond words can be helpful when dealing with deep pain and deep inquiry. Instead of writing your answers, you could draw them. Or you could ask a friend to be with you as you explore the questions. Or you could take the questions to a physical place that holds a challenging memory. Or you could use them to create a ritual for a new beginning.

Listen deeply. There's a lot of learning hidden in deep pain. We are continuously transformed by our lives. Let the dry spells and even the despair teach you about how to stay with your life through thick and thin. And remember, some seeds need darkness to sprout.

Dangers of Doubt

While we're exploring the darker side of transformation, I'd like to offer a few thoughts on doubt.

In many traditions, both spiritual and secular, doubt is considered a major hindrance to personal transformation. It's also unavoidable. Like dry spells and despair, doubt is going to show up now and then in your life. It's good to recognize it and recognize the subtle way it tries to undermine you. Here's an example:

A few years ago, I was riding high. ᴀɴᴅ had helped me reconcile so many tensions in my psyche and in my life. I was feeling vibrant and alive. I also seemed to have an expanded capacity to engage with a large constellation of meaningful things.

I had a renewed vigor in my work life. At my university, I was running a research lab, teaching my courses, and directing a campus-wide program to transform undergraduate education. Beyond the university, I was offering online and in-person workshops around the world. I was coaching and consulting on a variety of topics, from climate change to leadership development. I had just finished writing a Global Change Biology textbook and was ready for a new project.

And it felt *natural*. It was intense at times, but I felt a relaxed kind of focus. I wasn't working long hours, and I had plenty of time for other things in my life. I was spending great time with my kids and nourishing new friendships. I was also making lots of pottery and enjoying the solitude of my desert abode in New Mexico.

It was a far cry from the "hit in the head by a soccer goal" days. I felt confident but not cocky, pleased but not prideful. Or so I thought.

Earlier that year, I had been asked to apply for a senior leadership position at my university. If I'm being honest, the opportunity felt like a trap of tradeoffs. I'd be working long hours in a place I didn't really want to live for an institution that I had mixed feelings about.

And yet, the position itself was compelling. I had already been applying my OR-to-AND philosophy to institutional change. I had seen the power of AND to inspire individuals and groups. I had worked with small collaborative communities and big dysfunctional divisions. The new position would be an opportunity to scale up further and scale AND across the university.

I went ahead and applied, and after several rounds of interviews, I was one of the finalists.

Just before my last interview, a colleague pulled me aside and said, *"Bree, just for this hour, can you tell people what they want to hear?"*

At that moment, I knew that (a) Giving me the job would be too big of a risk for the university, and (b) Taking the job would be too big a risk for me. The job would put me on a bigger stage, but I'd be a smaller version of myself. I could no longer fit myself in a box.

Even so, I was devastated when I received the call saying that the search committee decided to give the job to the candidate who was a safer bet.

Why was I devastated to get passed over for a job that would have been terrible for me anyway?

One word: Doubt.

Doubt is the opposite of faith. The opposite of clarity. The opposite of trust.

When we are in doubt, our eyes are clouded—about ourselves, each other, and the world. We see lack and limitation, peril and pitfalls. We start asking the wrong kinds of questions like:

- What's wrong with me?
- What if I've irrevocably messed up?
- What if I never get another great opportunity?
- What if I stay lost forever?

In this case, instead of being grateful that I had newfound clarity in purpose and direction, I was fixated on the door that had closed. I couldn't see all the new possibilities that had been created.

When we face a setback, it's not only that we risk losing faith in ourselves. We also risk losing faith in the bigger picture.

Faith is a difficult concept for many people, but it's an essential ingredient in our lives. Even if you don't relate to the idea of faith in a spiritual sense, trusting *anything* can counteract the dangers of doubt.

You can trust yourself or your neighbor or your dog. You can trust the magic of timing or the mysteries of the universe or the flow of life itself. You can also trust AND to reemerge.

RSVP YES

The aftermath of the "tell them what they want to hear" interview process was hard. Not only was doubt clouding my mind, but I was also avoiding some glaring truths.

As the fog cleared, it became obvious what was happening.

I was grieving for the life I was leaving. The impact of AND on my life had been immense.

I was no longer the same person who had built a life around OR. Many of my closest relationships and strongest passions had evolved with me, and new opportunities kept emerging. Every time I let go of a commitment or relationship that felt irrevocably polluted by OR, something new and beautiful grew in its place.

And yet, I was still doing too much OR tourism—spending too much time in places ruled by fear and constraint. Sure, I could go to Berkeley and try to offer a breath of fresh air to my bedraggled students and colleagues. But I could no longer pretend I fit in my old life.

That's when I learned a deeper lesson about OR. OR is stingy and jealous and doesn't want you to make new friends or get fresh air.

I already knew that OR traffics in binaries—good or bad, right or wrong, friend or foe. What I didn't know was that OR would label me a foe for wanting a more joyful life.

Earlier, I cautioned you against self-help processes that sell a simple, linear "before" and "after." I also said that I don't love transformational frameworks based on a circular hero's journey. Yet, there is something the hero's journey gets right: *Coming home is hard.*

When we return from a journey bearing the fruits of our quest, it is nearly impossible to hide our "changed-ness." Even if we don't speak of our journey, we exude an independence that can feel threatening.

I had a poignant reminder of this one morning with my teenage son.

I had just returned from a trip to Europe. To everyone else in my life, it looked like a run-of-the-mill work trip. I gave a talk at a conference, facilitated a workshop, and spent a few days with dear colleagues. But to me, it was an enormous new beginning.

The months prior had been wonderful but challenging. After emerging from my fog of doubt, I had finally stepped away from a number of commitments and relationships that were constraining, both personally and professionally. The newfound freedom was exhilarating.

The trip to Europe felt like an affirmation that I had reunited with AND. In a single week, I had a flood of new personal and professional opportunities and a much deeper sense of being at home within myself. I wasn't yet getting magically matching phone and P.O. box numbers, but I was hearing the song of AND loud and clear.

That morning, my son and I were going about our typical routine of toasting bagels, feeding pets, and packing lunches. It was our ordinary world, but I was feeling an irrepressible joy.

BAGEL   APOLLO   ACORN   AND

Bodhi had been tossing the occasional "my mom is weird" look in my direction. Eventually, he stopped buttering his bagel, squared off, and said:

"Mom, can I RSVP "No" to whatever is happening with you right now?"

My first reaction was to laugh hysterically at how he phrased his question. My next response was, *"Wait, what? You can't be happy that your mom is happy?"*

Which is when he said, *"It's so much easier to have normal parents than happy parents."*

And that is when I remembered.

People don't like change, especially if it's change they can't control.

Every time we grow and change and transform and evolve, we are breaking the agreements that no longer serve us in our lives. We stop playing by the rules of an old game.

In reality, we are becoming more honest, more loving, and more true to ourselves.

But it might not look that way to others. When we break patterns and expectations, people sometimes get confused, judgmental, or angry. Misery loves company, as they say. It's one way OR tries to keep us in its clutches.

OR thinks it can criticize you back into compliance and conformity. Don't fall for it.

If you notice pushback from those in your life, here are a few things to remember:

Your transformation is *your* transformation. You need to do it your way, even if others don't understand.

You can't predict the exact effects of your journey. You need to have faith in yourself and the process.

The important people in your life can come along for the ride. If things get hard, remind them that they are invited on a grand adventure.

You may outgrow some people and places. That's okay. There will be plenty of amazing new horizons.

Evolution takes time. Play the long game, and don't micromanage people, places, or the process.

Actually, all of that can be summed up like this: *RSVP "YES."*

The best antidote to NO is always YES.

OR will try to seduce you into negativity by saying NO to who you are becoming. So, *RSVP "YES"* to yourself, your process, the challenges that arise, and the new horizons that emerge.

Standing strong in AND will not only enrich your own freedom but also will have ripple effects on those around you.

The wild happiness I felt that Bagel Morning was important to express, even if it confused my son. It was a moment of deepening my commitment to AND. I was unwilling to tamp down my joyful AND for someone else's stingy OR.

And that commitment was an invitation. I was, in effect, saying to Bodhi, "*I'm heading on a new adventure. Want to come along?*" That morning, he RSVP'd "*No.*" But the nice thing about AND invitations is that they don't expire.

Within a few months, Bodhi changed his RSVP and is now an enthusiastic companion in my new life.

It's wonderful to have people in your life say, "YES!" to your transformation. But *you* need to RSVP "YES" first. Only then does the invitation get put in the mail to others.

And if the mail gets lost or some guests refuse to join or your favorite goldfish dies on the day of the party, you can handle it.

And if ever you need a reminder that the challenges in your life have meaning and value, I have one more piece of advice to share... trust your struggle.

Trust Your Struggle

One of my favorite places in Oakland, California, is a small side street tucked behind Telegraph Avenue. It has a mural that is permanently painted in my mind.

The mural takes up the entire side of a building and depicts an ocean scene. There's a blue sky above, vibrant waves creating a horizon in the middle, and abstract yellow, white, and turquoise shapes under the water, which could be loosely interpreted as octopus tentacles.

In the middle of the scene—right above a door into the building—is a fully clothed woman walking nonchalantly through the ocean. She's submerged in water to her hips, walking through the bizarre underwater scene. Her stance is completely relaxed. She looks to the horizon with one hand dragging lazily through the water.

In the sky above her, huge looping letters say, "*Trust Your Struggle.*"

This phrase plays in my mind whenever I'm facing a particularly grueling cycle of transformation. It also comes out of my mouth quite often when I'm working with individuals or groups.

Sure, sometimes we need more support, more exercise, or more coffee. But sometimes, we just need to trust the struggle.

So, by all means, enjoy the "easy way" when it lands at your feet. But it's okay to sometimes take the "hard way." Evolution isn't always easy. The "hard way" can have powerful lessons. Being brought to our knees or lost in the dark is sometimes necessary for our growth and essential to our humanity.

Struggle without (at least a little) trust is brutal. Trust without (at least a bit of) struggle is superficial. Luckily, you're an AND-er. You can bring them together and *trust your struggle*.

&

CHAPTER 12

$\mathcal{A}ND$ as the Grand Connector

Make It Rain Harder

I recently took my kids to a Noah Kahan concert at the Greek Theatre in Berkeley. The Greek is an open-air amphitheater built in 1903, with concrete benches and carved stone seats cascading down an oak-filled hillside above the UC Berkeley campus.

I bought tickets almost a year prior, knowing the concert would be a few days after my daughter's return from her year in Spain. It would be a great midsummer celebration with my two teenagers.

As we waited for the show to begin, I reflected on how much had changed in our lives. When we lived in Berkeley together years ago, our lives were still so colored by OR. Now, we were visitors, passing through on our way to new AND horizons.

Noah's music had been a soundtrack during this transition. His songs are full of contrast: struggle and freedom, staying and leaving, destruction and renewal, nostalgia and hope, love and pain. He had unwittingly become a companion on our journey.

Eventually, the sun set, and the stage lights came on.

To raucous applause, Noah wheeled himself out on a knee scooter decorated with a festive strand of blue lights. Apparently, he had injured his leg earlier in the day and refused to cancel the concert.

He proceeded to sing his heart out and invent some exuberant one-legged dancing moves.

Watching Noah Kahan give his all in less-than-ideal circumstances reminded me of another iconic performance. In 2007, legendary musician Prince was slated to play the Super Bowl halftime show with an audience of 100,000 in the stadium and 100 million on live TV. It was pouring rain.

Shortly before the performance, the event producer called Prince.

He said, "*I want you to know it's raining.*"

Prince responded, "*Yes, it's raining.*"

The producer asked, "*And are you okay?*"

Prince countered, "*Can you make it rain harder?*"

Prince proceeded to give a tremendous performance punctuated by his turquoise dancing boots and signature opening of "*Dearly beloved, we are gathered here together to get through this thing called life."* Prince was not simply getting through this thing called life. He was dancing through an epic deluge.

Why am I telling you this as we come to the end of our time together?

Because these performances bear the signature of AND.

Instead of saying, *"Conditions must be right OR I will not perform,"* both Noah and Prince said, *"Conditions aren't perfect AND I will still give my all."* In fact, the setbacks (pouring rain and busted leg) set the stage for truly unique performances.

Great performers, great leaders, great builders, great pilots, great farmers, and great lovers interface with life *as it is.* **We don't wait on the sidelines until conditions are perfect. We dance with a busted leg or a broken heart. We sing in a gentle shower or a torrential downpour.**

"Can you make it rain harder?" isn't hubris or self-punishment. It's a bold acceptance of the circumstances.

So, go ahead. Stop waiting for conditions to be ideal. Look squarely at whatever limitations, frustrations, and setbacks you are facing. And decide to get on stage anyway.

Because, in the end, that's your primary decision. You don't get to choose your circumstances. But you do get to choose whether and how you participate. You can mope backstage with OR, drinking stale booze and glaring at the world through jaded and bloodshot eyes. Or you can dance with

AND, growing your courage, confidence, and capacity to interface with life as it is.

Once you're out on that dance floor, remarkable things start to happen.

Wisteria Reprise

Remember at the beginning of the book when I told you about getting hit in the head with a soccer goal?

I was living a life of OR and needed a wake-up call. After all, my teacher always cautioned that if Life taps you with a feather and you don't notice, Life will try to get your attention with a brick.

Once we are living with AND, we don't need the same kind of wake-up calls because we are already awake.

This isn't to say that we get inducted into some kind of enlightenment club. Nor is it a guarantee that we will avoid setbacks and pain. We will continue being human and having human experiences. Of course. But we will handle life with more curiosity, honesty, capacity, and grace.

And life responds to our newfound openness. Now, instead of getting hit with a brick, we may get handed a flower.

I remember the exact moment I realized how much had changed in my life thanks to AND. It was years after the Multidimensional Body class and years after the first AND-ers would eat chocolate in my living room. I had already started my rhythm of rotating between California, Colorado, and New Mexico, and I was in Berkeley to teach and offer a series of workshops.

On this particular day, I was hosting an eclectic class that integrated meditation and ceramics called "Pray in Clay." We were in my Berkeley backyard—the same garden where I had rested after being hit in the head with the soccer goal so many years before. I was sitting in the same simple wooden chair under the same enormous wisteria.

Wisteria is an amazing keeper of time. As years pass, wisteria grows. Our wisteria had now climbed to the top of the two-story house. The stems were as thick as tree trunks, the crown weighed several hundred pounds, and delicate purple flowers hung from every vine.

I was appreciating the play of the wisteria shadows on the ground and leading a guided meditation when... CRACK... there was a deafening sound immediately overhead.

An enormous section of the wisteria had broken and was falling down directly above me—limbs, leaves, and flowers plummeting from two stories high. I was about to get hit in the head. Again.

But this time, in the chaos that ensued, something in me stayed utterly still and completely calm. It's counterintuitive to stay still when vegetation is falling on your head, but I didn't move a muscle. I felt a wave of trust and some inexplicable guidance. *A tree is falling AND I must stay still.* I listened.

When the dust and leaves had settled, they revealed this: I was surrounded by wisteria debris, but the largest vine was nestled perfectly around me. There was an almost Bree-shaped curve in the branch. When the limb hit the ground on either side of me, the center was still perched a few inches above my head.

I can't tell you how or why the wisteria fell at that exact moment. But the lesson felt clear. When I wasn't listening to my life, I got hit on the head. When I was listening to my life, I got sprinkled with flowers. The difference wasn't between soccer goals and wisteria branches. The difference was in my listening.

Our listening affects not just our inner experience but also the outer outcomes of our lives. With the Soccer Goal Incident, I needed months to recover from a debilitating brain injury. With the Wisteria Incident, I needed just moments to gather myself.

I'm not saying that being spared by the wisteria was proof of some kind of magical protection. I'm still flesh and bones and subject to all the associated joys and pains.

What I am saying is that AND gives us the capacity to listen, chart a more joyful life, and respond in real time to the unexpected.

AND aligns us with our deeper truth and attracts positive potentiality into our lives. AND brings more flowers and fewer bruises. In contrast, OR magnetizes conflict and challenge. OR keeps us fixated on fear and attracts more negative outcomes into our lives.

This isn't a mysterious or woo-woo process. It's all about what we are listening to and where we are putting our attention.

Listen to What You Know

We talked at the beginning of our journey about knowing the *tone* of OR versus AND. You can trust yourself to *hear* the difference between a stingy OR and a generous AND in your thoughts and in your life.

I'd also like you to trust the *feel* of your journey. You can trust yourself to navigate by your *sense* of the currents in your life. *Feelings* are different than emotions. They have a deeper origin and are an innate inner compass.

Let's look at the *feel* of AND and how to trust it.

In the last chapter, we talked about how to trust your struggle when things are dark. Struggle is necessary, even if it isn't pleasant. It also has a very clear *feel*. For me, struggle feels like a cocktail of fear, pressure, conflict, and urgency. It feels like I'm simultaneously being collapsed in and ripped out. I feel lost at sea—like I can't catch my breath between the battering waves.

It may be a little different for you, but there's a *feel* to struggle. Knowing that feeling will help you get your bearings and make appropriate choices. Instead of frantically flailing for a breath, you might look around for a lifeboat or orient yourself with the currents to get to shore.

We have an equal need to *feel* during times of ease. Even if things feel relatively smooth, there's still motion, current, and orientation. Even when your hands seem to be off the wheel, there's a deep kind of navigation happening. You're still participating in the currents of life.

So, I also want you to be able to *trust your trust*.

I know that sounds slightly absurd, but it's not. Trust has its very own *feel*. For me, trust feels open, warm, solid, and light. Trust is very intimate and personal yet also expansive and universal. Trust simultaneously contains a deep knowing and a deep not-knowing. Trust feels like the ocean being the ocean.

Why is this important?

Because we live in a time and culture where we pay attention to loud things, which is why OR holds so much sway in our lives. OR grabs our attention and holds it with fear and negativity. OR cajoles, criticizes, commands, and confines. It's loud enough to hear above the background noise.

In contrast, the song of AND is quiet. It requires our *conscious attention*. We need to seek out the feeling of trust to get to know it. Once we have taken the time to know our inner compass, it will guide us faithfully. But we have to cut through the noise to get there.

One of my favorite examples of this principle comes from a long-ago student, Ben, who was in the first "weird" course I offered at Berkeley.

One day, I was trying to describe the *feel* of intuition to a group of highly skeptical scientists when I remembered an activity from the Multidimensional Body class. The Doc and Rev had seated us blindfolded in a circle and passed around a series of objects. We simply needed to track our feelings of resonance or repulsion when each object arrived. The point wasn't to decide which specific objects we liked or didn't like. The point was to *feel* our inner "yes" or inner "no."

I adapted the activity to the moment and tried it with my class. I passed around a rock, a crumpled scrap of paper, a piece of chalk, a tube of ChapStick, a plastic figurine, and a tiny clay bowl.

The students were quiet with closed eyes as we passed the objects around our makeshift circle. Then, when they could see each other again, I had the students summarize how they felt about each object with a simple thumbs-up or thumbs-down.

When we debriefed the activity, these were their observations:

No one lacks an inner compass. Everyone had strong, clear feelings about the objects immediately upon contact. Even the students who considered themselves to be indecisive or out-of-touch with themselves had at least one clear "yes" and at least one obvious "no."

A *feeling* is more trustworthy than an *opinion*. Students couldn't predict their feelings based on preconceived opinions. They said things like, "*I can't stand plastic. Why did I love that ChapStick?*" or "*I love nature. Why did I cringe at the rock?*" Ultimately, feelings win. It matters how you *actually* feel, not how you think you *should* feel.

Intuition is preciously subjective. There were no universally loved or despised objects, none that always got a thumbs up or a thumbs down. People have different preferences and resonances. Just because you like the feel of a tiny plastic figurine doesn't mean I will. No one else can reliably predict *your* intuition.

Trust requires listening and practice. Even when students had a clear "yes" or 'no," they didn't always trust it. You need to practice listening—and taking action—based on your feelings. Every time you listen to yourself, your access to intuition gets stronger.

The same principles apply to the mundane and the monumental. If you can trust your "yes" and your "no" about small things, you can do the same with big things. You can make real-life decisions based on your inner sense of resonance. When I ignored my "no" about the cat rescue, it didn't end well. When I listened to my "yes" about the round house, a lifetime of adventure opened.

Since that day with the rock, ChapStick, and crumpled paper, I've facilitated this activity for hundreds of people around the world. The conclusion is always the same. *Everyone has an inner knowing. We just need to listen.*

Let's come back to Ben.

At the time, I didn't know that Ben had a kind of intuition awakening during this activity. He didn't stay after class, and he didn't mention how much he loved the rock we passed around the circle. But many years later, he stopped by my office to tell me he was getting married. He was recounting the story of meeting his future wife when he paused; his eyes got bright, and he said:

"You know, Bree. It was exactly the same feeling as that rock you passed around the circle. I always remembered the feeling of that rock. It felt like YES. That's exactly how it felt to meet her."

This isn't a story about love at first sight. It's a story about trust. You can trust *yourself* to live on your own terms. And you can trust the *feeling* of YES to help you navigate your life.

The way we *find* our YES is by *listening to what we know*. The way we *follow* our YES is by *looking where we want to go*.

The best way to illustrate this final point is with a lesson in motorcycle riding.

Look Where You Want to Go

If you learn to ride a motorcycle, one piece of advice that you will hear again and again is: *Look where you want to go*.

Novice bikers tend to fixate on trying to avoid danger. The problem is that by focusing your gaze on the cone, pedestrian, or truck you want to avoid, you are actually more likely to hit it. Your eyes zero in on the scary or dangerous parts of the landscape, and your body follows.

In contrast, an expert rider knows how to stay relaxed and look toward the horizon. When you relax your gaze and look further ahead, you naturally take in the entire landscape. You trust your body to respond if there's a curve, car, or deer in the road. Your relaxation actually keeps you safer.

Novice and expert riders may cruise through the exact same landscape, but they *see it differently*. **The novice sees dangers to avoid and is focused by anxiety. The expert sees the beauty of the ride and stays alert and engaged without fear.**

This isn't just about having a more pleasant experience on the bike. It's also about outcomes. The scared rider is more likely to crash and burn.

The same is true in our lives.

When we are trapped in OR, we are like novice bikers. Our vision narrows, we obsess over our fears, and we see only a small sliver of the landscape of our lives. We think our vigilance is protecting us, but it is actually a grave liability. When "bad" things happen, we don't see that our fear and fixation are the culprits.

When we are tapped into AND, we are expert riders. We are relaxed and open, we take life as it comes, and we trust ourselves to navigate the complex landscape of our lives. When challenging situations arise, we deal with them in real time and keep moving. We are less likely to judge outcomes as "bad" because we see the big picture and our need to learn from all types of experiences.

Here's a literal example. The other day, Jake was riding his motorcycle on the small local highway connecting Taos to Tres Piedras, New Mexico. He was going fast but was relaxed, open, and looking where he wanted to go. All of a sudden, a turkey appeared, flapping out of nowhere. Jake ducked and felt the massive bulk brush against his helmet, where his head had been an instant prior.

Taking a twenty-pound bird in the face while driving a motorcycle at highway speeds could have catastrophic outcomes. Instead, it was a brief moment of surprise followed by a nice, long sunset ride.

So, here's another invitation from AND. Look where you want to go and trust yourself to respond in real time to your life. You don't need to stress about all the orange traffic cones you're trying to avoid. You don't need to take a twenty-pound turkey in the face. And you certainly don't need to use fear to focus your mind.

You've got lots of resources now. You know the cost of OR. You feel the benefit of AND. You have a method to transform fear into possibility. You also have a bonus superpower, which is this:

Living a life of openness and possibility is actually a type of homecoming. You're returning to your natural state. The truth of AND has a gravitational pull.

You just need to look where you want to go: *Home.*

Your Birthright

Let me put on my biologist hat one final time. For me, biology isn't just the study of life. It's the study of connection.

I see connections *everywhere*, not because I'm wearing rose-colored glasses, but because I have studied life on this planet for decades. My research has taken me to deserts, mountains, and rainforests around the world. My work ranges in scale from the molecular to the planetary and traverses the tree of life from microbes to mammals. When I distill nearly thirty years of studying our planet, I come to a simple and undeniable conclusion:

Connection is perhaps the most fundamental principle of existence.

We live on a planet teeming with life. Millions of species are engaged at every moment in an intricate dance of interdependence. Predators, pollinators, producers, and even parasites are all essential in our earthly web of life. A tree doesn't exist without worms in the soil and birds in the canopy. And *you* don't exist without connection at every level of your being.

The very blueprint of your life is built on connection. In the innermost sanctum of your cells, trillions of bonds hold strands of your DNA together. And your cells themselves are the result of an ancient merging of previously distinct life forms. You wouldn't exist if your nuclei and mitochondria hadn't established a historic cooperation.

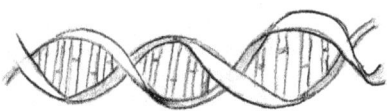

You also wouldn't exist if the trillions of different cells in your body weren't able to coordinate thousands of complex functions. In your brain alone, tens of billions of neurons create a hundred trillion connections seamlessly without you even noticing.

And speaking of cells, the cells that are "yours" make up far less than 50 percent of the cells in your body. By some estimates, our bodies contain ten times as many microbial cells as human cells, representing thousands of types of bacteria, fungi, and viruses. Some of these are pathogens, but the vast majority are silently performing essential functions that sustain your life.

You are not an individual. You are an ecosystem. You are forged by connection at every level of your being.

In fact, it's very difficult to tell exactly where "you" begin and end.

Sure, you have a membrane of skin that protects you from the elements. But the air you breathe, the food you eat, and the life forms you host are essential for your survival.

Whether you're an introvert or an extrovert, an influencer or a monk, you are irrevocably connected. There is no way to keep a safe distance from life; you are already in the dance.

Everything that makes our lives possible is the result of bringing together disparate things. Nature is a network of interconnection and interdependence. Nature isn't made up of straight lines and tight boxes. *We* are the ones who artificially divide things.

We take a universe of AND, and we carve out little fiefdoms of OR. We divide *this from that, here from there,* and *us from them.* We do this to give ourselves a sense of security or stability in an almost unfathomably complex world.

We create divisions to our own great peril. Our OR mentality has led us to the brink of social, political, and ecological collapse.

The power of AND is thus not only important in our individual lives but also in our collective endeavors. Our families, our communities, our institutions, our societies, our ecosystems, and our planet all desperately need us to come home to the reality of connection.

There is a simple choice to make. We have the power to create divisions and live in a greedy, stingy OR world. We also have the power to build connections and live in a world of great and generous possibility.

Simple choices are not always easy. And connection is not always easy. Is it easy for your heart to pump thousands of gallons of blood each day? Is it easy for plankton to produce gigatons of oxygen each year? Is it easy for our universe to continuously form new stars beyond the reaches of our measurement?

Truly, I have no idea. Even if these things aren't easy, they are still true. Truth isn't measured by ease. Truth is measured by truth.

Connection is our birthright—it's written into the very biology, chemistry, and physics of our lives. Whether it feels easy or not, you can always choose truth.

The reality of connection is there for you. AND is happy to share endless examples of connection at work in your life and in the cosmos. All you need to do is listen.

The Great Connector

In its simplest grammatical form, And is a conjunction. A connector. And connects different sentences, divergent ideas, disparate people, and diverse possibilities.

And has no limits. And doesn't put its foot down and refuse to bridge a sentence because the clauses are too dissimilar. And doesn't turn its back on topics that are difficult or deep. And doesn't scoff at ideas that seem especially playful or puckish.

And signed up for it all.

You can, too.

Sure, it sounds great to connect *love And light*, but it's also possible to connect *roses And rage* or *pain And peonies*. Allowing seemingly disparate things to coexist will help you craft a more honest, creative, and courageous life.

It will also have ripple effects.

Once you start living with And, you will have a much greater capacity for nuance and truth. You will see the world more honestly. You will no longer demand false consistency from yourself or others.

Your life will have more inner coherence because you aren't hiding things from yourself. Your relationships will have more depth because you aren't demanding that others hide aspects of themselves in your presence. And your rapport with the world will be infinitely more grounded and compassionate because you're interfacing with things as they really are.

Because, in the end, AND is a choice about the way you see and interact with life.

When it's pouring rain, you can bemoan your ruined concert, or you can get on stage and give your all. When it's raining wisteria, you can run and hide, or you can listen for guidance. When it's pelting turkeys, you can wipe out on the gravel or keep your eyes on the horizon.

You don't always choose your circumstances, but you do choose how you engage with life.

So go ahead and sprinkle a bit more AND into your life. Every time you do, the cosmic scales tip a bit more toward possibility, creativity, and joy.

And remember, you already have some big weights on the AND side of the scale.

You have your natural intuition for AND. You know the sound of AND's voice because it's been a quiet friend your entire life. Your existence is built on connection. It's your biological birthright.

You also have a specific method to shift your thinking and living from OR to AND. You can start a daily OR-to-AND practice or just lean on the four questions when you need them. Regardless, you have a foundation, a process, and a wealth of practices you can return to again and again.

Finally, you have support. You've got these pages, a companion guided journal if you'd like more prompts and inspiration, plus ways of staying connected on my website. AND you've got each other. There's a whole world of

AND-ers out there. Some of them just might not know it yet. So, invite folks into the club.

AND won't give you a nifty certificate of completion because the journey continues. But AND loves a goofy membership card and a snappy T-shirt. Carry yours with pride.

No End

This book is about to end, but not really. Your journey with AND has no static endpoint. After all, you're beyond lines and boxes now.

Sure, there will still be pressures to conform, and you no longer need to dwell on them.

You don't want to live a scripted life. You don't want a fake formula pretending to solve all your problems. You don't want to play a dead-end game by someone else's rules.

Instead, you're ready to look where you want to go.

If your curvy AND journey could take you anywhere at all, where would you like to go? What do you really want for your life?

You don't need to draw inside the lines. And you don't have to pick a single destination. Even if you choose AND as your North Star, you can still make millions of constellations.

Now that you're an AND-er, you get to call on the power of AND to fuel your journey.

AND is a small word, but it's got serious might. When you summon the power of AND, you will automatically create new possibilities in your life. You will naturally build new connections with yourselves, others, and the world. You will easily spread love and paella.

So go ahead. Celebrate a new beginning with the curvy little ampersand that's ready to dance into your life.

AND is a great connector, and now you are too.

With love,

Special Th&nks

Earlier this year, I was writing a book. *This* wasn't it. *That* book was well-planned, thoughtfully considered, and drew on years of my writing.

Then, six months before "AND" went to press, I was inspired—or rather *compelled*—to shift gears entirely and let this book emerge—on its own terms.

I told you about my conversation with Jake at the Maple Bacon diner in Texas. But what I didn't tell you is that right after that conversation, I just couldn't shake the feeling that AND needed a book *NOW*.

So, I scrapped the book I had already developed and RSVP'd "YES" to this one.

Writing a book is nothing like giving birth. But the metaphor is used often. Both of my children were born after long, slow labors. So, I know how to run the metaphorical marathon when birthing new things. But *this* book had no interest in prenatal yoga, lavender baths, or a Pitocin drip. This book wanted to jump out dancing.

It takes love, trust, and support to write a book, more so to write a book *quickly*. So, thank you:

Jake, always and because. I'm looking forward to the next book in so many ways.

Chloe and Bodhi, for being remarkable, fun, creative, and resilient. It's hard to be kids with a weird mom, especially when you end up on journeys you might have preferred to skip. This book is, in many ways, about *our* journey, and I'm so grateful that you're on it with me. I'll always pack pretzels.

Jordan, my talented brother, for agreeing to do one last design project before sailing his boat to new horizons. Thank you for a dynamite book design and an extraordinary lifelong friendship.

Rev. Zoe Inman and Dr. Eric Rubin, for offering lifelines of wisdom that run through this book and my life. You woke up seeds of possibility in my heart and taught me how to nourish them.

Wendy and Mark, for not rounding off my strange edges. Mom, you were a key support in the Oʀ years, and you're always willing to look at Life under the microscope together—thank you.

Jeanne, for remarkably tending the beauty, mystery, and love. And, Gigi, for dancing with us on the grand adventure.

Rachel, for *really* getting it and staying through thick and thin.

Kristen, for always helping me see the bigger AND on the horizon.

Leslie, for being a fabulous lab partner (which is high praise from a scientist) and for your willingness to experiment and nourish seeds of possibility.

Carlos, for bringing the poetry of the infinite back to the fore.

Ari, for captaining an amazing submarine, which always brings back pearls from the depths.

PC, whose dogged commitment to creativity inspired new directions in my life. (I just had no idea this would be one of them.)

Dear friends who offered feedback on the book as it was peeking its furry head into the world: Chloe, Jake, Jordan, Rachel, Laura, Allie, Carlos, and Hope. And many dear friends and mentors who were part of this journey from behind the scenes: Seema, Janel, Robin, Tamara, Todd, Roland, Tara, Luke, Li, and Len.

Nicole, Kim, Tami, and the entire team at Niche Pressworks, whose commitment to independence and integrity is palpable in everything they do. Thanks especially to Julie and Anna for their grounded and insightful feedback throughout.

AND-ers through all space and time. This book is for you, and I'm grateful to you for being part of the journey.

About the Author

Bree Rosenblum is a Professor and Distinguished Chair at UC Berkeley, an organizational consultant, a motivational speaker, and a workshop facilitator. Her work has been featured broadly in the press, including the *New York Times*, *National Geographic*, the Discovery Channel, National Public Radio, the BBC movie *Endangered*, and on the TEDx stage. *AND* isn't just the title of this book; it's her life philosophy. Bree weaves her work on the biodiversity of our planet with her passion for supporting others on the journey of life. She draws on an eclectic history as a professor, meditation teacher, organizational leader, potter, climber, roving naturalist, and art nerd. Bree received her BA from Brown University and her PhD from UC Berkeley. She lives in New Mexico, Colorado, California, and wherever AND takes her. You can find her at BreeRose.com.

Looking for ways to stay in touch?

We could all use a little more AND in our lives. Here are some ways you can spread that tiny—yet mighty—word...

Join Bree's mailing list. Be the first to receive bonus material, event announcements, and workshop invitations.

Pick up the AND companion journal. Deepen your journey with a guided journal dedicated to helping AND come alive in your life.

Share AND with friends, colleagues, and community members. Introduce AND to others—whether for a birthday, book club or business retreat—with discounts on bulk orders.

Schedule Bree as a keynote. Select from a slate of inspirational talks—or work with Bree to customize an event for your audience.

Donate to Bree's non-profit. Help build the Hearth Institute—a retreat center in northern New Mexico dedicated to supporting personal and organizational transformation.

More information on these and other AND invitations at...
www.BreeRose.com